Dedication

This book is dedicated to the doubting Thomas's of this world. I know God has a special place in His heart for you.

A Real God in an Unreal World

Barry Raeburn

Barry Raeburn Evangelistic Association
Tulsa, Oklahoma

A Real God in an Unreal World
Published by:
Barry Raeburn Evangelistic Association
8988-L South Sheridan, Suite 254
Tulsa, Oklahoma 74133
ISBN 978-0-9820967-0-3

Cover design and book production by:
Silver Lining Creative
www.silverliningcreative.com
Cover illustration is protected by the 1976 United States Copyright Act.
Copyright © 2008 by Silver Lining Creative

Printed in the United States of America.

Contents

Chapter 1
Let Me Be Real with You

Wait! Wait, just a moment, and before you put this book down and relegate the contents to yet another feeble attempt by another narrow-minded Christian to convince you of the truths of the claims of Christianity, I want you to take some time to skim read the contents. Maybe, just maybe you will find something, which is meaningful to you. Maybe you will find some of what I have written has relevance to your life.

What I am writing is from the heart, from one human being to another. I'm asking you to take a few moments to consider the contents and evaluate them for yourself. If you are not interested that is fine, but maybe you will find something that inspires you to have an encounter with God. My goal is to introduce you to the One who created you. I don't think that it's an unworthy goal. You deserve a chance to meet God. Everyone should.

Words can communicate what is on the heart. My greatest desire is to introduce you to a new reality, the reality of God. It is my hope that what I am about to write may be able to reach out to you from these pages and have a profound impact on you. I feel a tremendous sense of responsibility. It is as if I have been entrusted with a treasure, which is beyond human comprehension, and feel a pressing need to share this treasure with you.

If you could only see what I have seen and experience what I have experienced, if you could meet God the way I have, you would know what I'm talking about. I have set for myself the impossible task of convincing you of the existence of God, but in my attempt to do this I am persuaded that God Himself will move heaven and earth to prove to you He is real. As I share, I know God will use what is shared to reveal Himself to you.

Let me share some things with you about the world we live in. It is my belief that we live in an unreal world. A world, which we like to think is real and full of hope for life, but I want to argue it is a world of emptiness; it is not all it claims to be. It is my firmly held conviction that if you have never experienced the reality of God you will never truly know just how unreal this world is.

In this world, people strive so hard to find some measure of satisfaction, but in their hearts, they are never truly satisfied. They may feel happy sometimes, but in the deepest part of their souls, they are not truly happy. It is a world where people hunger for things, which ultimately make them more hungry, and where they thirst for things, which ultimately make them more thirsty.

There is a cry in the inmost heart of every human being, "there must be something more to life!" People may never say anything to their friends or family but their heart is saying, "there must be more! There must be something more than the struggle to be king of the mountain; to die with the most toys; to have a happy family and good friends; to live like the Jones'." Some of these things may be good and worthy achievements, but they still leave people with that restless feeling, there must be more.

When we look at the world we live in, sometimes we think to ourselves "someone must have created all this," and we say to ourselves, "where did it all come from?"

"How could all of this beauty and complexity be here just by chance?" We wonder "is there a God out there somewhere?" The reason I'm writing this book is to make the bold and confident statement that "God is alive." I am an eyewitness to the reality of the living God. I had this cry in my heart. I had asked all these questions and I can assure you from personal experience, God is there.

Even though there are people who claim to have met God, our world seems separated from the reality of God. It denies the existence of God. How can this be? God is more real than any of us can possibly imagine. People continue to live their lives as though He does not exist. Their lives seem untouched by the reality of God, and yet God is alive! How can this be explained? It is unthinkable that if God is truly alive that some people have not yet met Him.

There must be some way for every person on the face of this planet to meet with God. He created every one of us. Not having the opportunity to meet with God is like a child having no opportunity to meet their parents! When you meet God, you meet the One who created you. There is nothing more special than that and yet, many never get the opportunity. In my humble opinion, this is the greatest tragedy of the human race.

Meeting with God will change your life! There is something about meeting with Him, which I liken to tasting the finest food. Once you have tasted it, nothing else satisfies you anymore, you become a person spoiled for anything less than the very best. Things that may have excited you in the past, don't excite you any more.

One of the early church fathers, the Apostle Paul had been impacted by God in a profound way. He said everything he had experienced and succeeded at in life was refuse and waste compared to his experience with God.

3

He would give them up in a heartbeat in order to be with God (Philippians 3:8). The Apostle Paul was a great theologian and was esteemed highly in his community as a teacher, as a Pharisee. All his accomplishments meant nothing to him when he compared them with his experience of God.

Meeting God changes everything. Once you meet God you realize that only God can give you true peace, true happiness, true life. Life presents these things to us, but what we experience of these things in our unreal world is really just a shadow of the reality that can be experienced with God. Only God is real. God and His reality is more real than the unreal world we live in.

God listens to our every thought and every heart's cry. Jesus said God hears our prayers even before we ask. He knows our inmost thoughts. God is watching you and listening to you as you read this book. He is examining your heart and life. He is waiting for the right moment to introduce Himself to you. If you will keep an open mind and an open heart, God will make Himself real to you.

God is real and yet this world is full of so much pain, sadness and misery. When he saw the condition of humanity Mahatma Gandhi commented "there are people in the world so hungry, that God cannot appear to them except in the form of bread."[1] God knows that there is so much pain in this life and so much misery. He wants to come in the form of bread to those who are starving. He wants to do miracles to meet the needs we have, to bring His Spirit to our lives, and convert our ashes and ruin into something wonderful.

God did just that for me, he came into my life as the miracle I needed. As part of my efforts to be real with you, I want to share my own experience with God. It will help you understand where I am coming from, why I am so convinced of God's existence and provide a point of reference for the statements I make concerning the reality of God.

In the third chapter, I describe God and you need to understand where I have come from to know how I can do that with any semblance of sincerity and authenticity. I believe God knew what I needed to convince me of His existence and that God can do the same for you.

Chapter 2
The Encounter

I had the privilege of growing up in a Christian home. I was taught the fundamental truths of Christianity and had a limited experience with the reality of God. My faith, although fragile remained intact until I reached university. At college I made my escape from what I perceived was a guilt-ridden religion.

At college, I was taught that humans had created religion to help deal with the seemingly unexplainable mysteries of the universe. At college, I conveniently exchanged my faith in Christianity for a combination of agnosticism and new age philosophy.

I believed that much of what Christianity claimed to be as a spiritual experience could be explained away as being psychologically induced. These *weak* people, I reasoned, *needed* religion. It was their crutch and way of coping with life, while we more intelligent advanced and educated people didn't need this type of help.

I think I must have broken my poor mother's heart when I sat in our lounge at home and sincerely explained to her that I did not believe in heaven or hell or sin, or any other of Christianity's guilt ridden concepts. I proceeded to tell her that not only did I not believe in God, but that I was god! (In the New Age sense).

In my unbelief, I was never willing to deny the possibility that God existed. I felt it was intellectually dishonest and that there was too much evidence in the earth and the universe for a creator, intelligent designer, infinite mind or whatever designation you might want to give such a being. I would always say to God, if You are out there and You can prove to me beyond any shadow of doubt that You exist, then I will believe. The rational arguments and debates I had with Christian friends would not sway me at all.

It was in my second year of college that I saw a poster advertising a miracles meeting at a local church. I thought it might be fun to go along and see what would happen. Maybe I would see a miracle or God might show up. I went to the meeting held at Hamilton Assemblies of God Church. The speaker was an Australian healing evangelist by the name of Tim Hall.

Tim preached a message on tenacity, hanging on to God and not letting go. Towards the end of the meeting, he began to describe a number of situations concerning people's lives. He pointed in my direction and said there is a young man sitting in this direction, he has been into drugs, he is confused, and he needs to come up to the front.

I felt my heart begin to thump in my chest and I looked around. There were old people everywhere, and I could not see anyone who might fit this preacher's description. I thought he must have been talking about me. I can honestly say, the only reason I went up to the front was because I wanted to know how he knew I was there. Was it some sort of party trick or had God actually spoken to him? If God had spoken to him, I wanted to know how.

We went through what I perceived was the usual drill, praying the sinners prayer (which I did not pray, because I knew it already). Then we went out the back with our counselors. The counselor I had was a nice man, very gentle and kind. He showed me through the Billy Graham Steps to God Booklet. I told him I was just really messed up and that I already knew the Gospel message. I just wanted to know how this man had known I was in the meeting. I really wanted to find out and understand whether God had spoken to him.

The counselor said "why don't we get him to pray for you?" I agreed. We went out the front and the counselor explained to the evangelist that I was the young man who was confused, and had been into drugs and so forth. Tim said, "lift your hands" and I thought, "why not? I'll give anything a try." I lifted my hands and he began to shout out a number of times "Spirit of God" it seemed like he was shouting out to God for me. After he did this a few times for some reason I thought, this guy actually believes there is a God. I felt like a little crack formed in my mind.

I also felt something stirring in or around my stomach and I thought, I don't want to miss this so I looked down and I saw with the naked eye, what seemed to be a beam of light coming into my stomach area. The beams increased until it was like a stream of light coming into me. I thought to myself I can't be imagining this, in all honesty it was the last thing I would have thought of in terms of "psychologically inducing" something.

I wasn't visualizing it, or imagining it, I was actually seeing it with my physical eyes, and my mind was analyzing it. I was in shock actually, wondering what was happening. In my previous hallucinatory experiences I knew they originated in my mind, but this was different. I was encountering a spiritual reality which I knew was an objective reality, a spiritual realm.

The stream just seemed to stop after a while and I felt this light starting from my feet slowly rising up my body and it begin to fill me. It rose and when it reached my head, it pushed out all the false ideology and messed up drug-induced confusion. For a while I stood there and I felt like I was floating about four feet off the floor. I felt like I was in heaven. I turned to the counselor and he said, "Do you believe in God now?" It took me a long while to respond and God knows I struggled in that moment, because in all honesty, I didn't want to, but I replied, "I guess I have to."

With respect to my conversion experience, I have always identified with the experience of C.S. Lewis. The great Christian author and former fervent atheist said that God had to drag him kicking and screaming into the Kingdom of God every step of the way. He said "you must picture me alone in that room in Magdalen, night after night, feeling, whenever my mind lifted even for a second from my work, the steady, unrelenting approach of Him whom I so earnestly desired not to meet. That which I greatly feared had at last come upon me. In the Trinity Term of 1929 I gave in, and admitted that God was God, and knelt and prayed: perhaps, that night, the most dejected and reluctant convert in all of England."[2]

This is what it was like for me. I'm sure I was the most reluctant convert in all of New Zealand, and to this day there are issues I struggle with, with respect to the claims of Christianity, but in a moment of time I knew God was real, I knew the Bible was true and I knew sin was real. I knew I had to give my *issues* to God and allow Him to help me come to an understanding of things in time.

It's amazing what a miracle will do that no amount of persuasion could ever do. There was part of me that still didn't want to believe that God existed, because I still had so many objections to God and another part which was so awestruck with what I had seen and experienced that I was convinced God was real. This experience with God transformed my life forever. God was real and there was no way to deny His existence, no matter how much I wanted to.

From that moment, I began my life as a believer. I discovered God was someone far more beautiful and wonderful than I could have ever dreamed of or imagined. I was spoiled for anything less than His presence. I had to spend all my time talking with Him and praying. I witnessed to all of my friends and led some of them to Christ. I spent hours reading the scriptures and spending time learning from God through prayer.

I remember being invited at the time to attend the management ball. Previously this would have been the highlight of the year, being there with all the best of the best people, all successful, but compared to what I had experienced, it all seemed very empty. I should have been so happy, but I was miserable, all I wanted was more of God. I wanted that taste of the supernatural, I had an insatiable thirst for God.

A thought that struck me at the time was "why doesn't everyone know about this?" I soon came to realize that this is the world we live in. People don't know God exists and that He is alive. Many have been led to believe that if God is there, He is judgmental and while it is true we are sinners, nobody emphasizes the beauty, love and splendor of God to those who have never met Him. The church and those who claim to know God often misrepresent Him to others. I believe that we can listen to what

11

others tell us about God, but we need to experience God for ourselves, to really know what He is like.

The God I met was totally different to anything I could have imagined. Previously I was focused on God's demand for loyalty and obedience, I believed God or religion certainly was all about sin and judgment. The God I met was breathtaking. To this day, I just can't describe to you how beautiful God is.

I just wanted to live to please Him because He was awe-inspiring and I would never want anything that would cause Him pain. I had objected to a God who made so many demands and yet when I met Him, He was totally otherworldly and beautiful. In truth I was happy; God's beauty had stolen my heart.

I remember a few months after I had come to Christ, I found a place to stay at a Youth With a Mission base. This was a place where missionaries lived and operated from. It was an incredible place, with so many people dedicated to serving God. I was praying in my room and I felt God come and visit me and He was so close. I saw a great light and I was overwhelmed with the reality and presence of God.

After prayer, I went downstairs and there was a man in the lounge who was asking questions. I went over to find out what had been happening and he had been walking down the street past the base and had seen a great light over the building. I was able to spend time sharing with this man what the great light was. God is able to be seen by the naked eye, and no one can convince me otherwise. This man saw something! He wanted to know what it was! God can show Himself to you, I have no doubt.

On another occasion I was praying in the living room of a friend's house. I cried out to God, "God I need to see you. I can't live like this anymore, I have to meet with you." I continued to cry out to God and then I saw what seemed to be a great cloud coming into the ceiling of the living room. I said to God "right...now I have you here I have a question for you." At the time I didn't know what the question was, but I knew I had to ask it. Finally, I said to God, "What is it like being God?" I felt God say, "It's so wonderful." Then His presence lifted.

I thought about this response and thought, "yes it must be wonderful being God." It was not like God was on some kind of power trip, happy that He was in charge of everything. He was trying to show me that He was having a good time all the time and that I didn't need to have such a negative view of Him. God created all the universe and all the beautiful things in it. He looked at everything He made and saw that it was good. I believe He enjoyed creating everything.

God enjoys being God. It's wonderful being God. We think God must be burdened down and troubled by all the things He is responsible for, but the Bible tells us that God thinks differently.

For my thoughts are not your thoughts, neither are your ways my ways, declares the LORD.

As the heavens are higher than the earth, so are my ways higher than your ways and my thoughts than your thoughts.
Isaiah 55:8,9

We think God thinks the way we do, but God's thoughts are so much higher than ours, and He lives in the realm of beauty, He is the most beautiful being you can possibly imagine.

Many people have ideas in their head as to what God is like or what heaven is like, they say things like "when I get to heaven I will play golf, or some other activity they really enjoy." I just don't believe God is like that and I don't believe heaven is like that. When I came to the Lord, my Pastor, Ian McCormack had the testimony that he had died and been to heaven and been brought back to life again miraculously. When I first met him I felt like he was looking right through me; I could tell his experience had transformed him and his view of reality. You could just tell he had been to heaven.

I can guarantee you this Pastor doesn't believe he will be spending his time in heaven playing golf. He said in heaven he saw Jesus and His face shone with light. As he walked towards Jesus he wasn't able to see his face because the light was too overwhelming and bright. This Pastor's face shone with the presence of God as he shared his story. He has shared his story all around the world. This is what an encounter with God will do to you. God is not about entertaining us with earthly pursuits, He is entirely different than we can imagine and heaven is an entirely different place than we can envision.

Throughout history God has revealed Himself to different people. Many times God came and appeared to people as a fire and a great cloud of glory. When God delivered the children of Israel out of the land of Egypt, He led them to a mountain. He appeared to all the people on that mountain and Moses went up into the presence of God.

The description of this is found in Exodus 19:18:

Mount Sinai was covered with smoke, because the LORD descended on it in fire. The smoke billowed up from it like smoke from a furnace, the whole mountain trembled violently.

14

In 2 Chronicles 7 when King Solomon dedicated the temple he had built, God appeared to all of the people in a similar way:

> **When Solomon finished praying, fire came down from heaven and consumed the burnt offering and the sacrifices, and the glory of the LORD filled the temple.**
>
> **The priests could not enter the temple of the LORD because the glory of the LORD filled it.**
>
> **When all the Israelites saw the fire coming down and the glory of the LORD above the temple, they knelt on the pavement with their faces to the ground, and they worshiped and gave thanks to the LORD, saying, "He is good; his love endures forever."**
>
> **2 Chronicles 7:1-3**

These people saw something which caused a reaction in their lives! When you see God it does something to you. When I think back on my encounter with God it still shakes me to think that I actually saw God. This kind of bare faced encounter with God will do something to you. Moses walked into the presence of God. He talked with God face to face.

The Bible tells us that the face of Moses shone when he had been in the presence of God, so much so that he had to wear a veil over his face so the people wouldn't be afraid of him.

> **When Aaron and all the Israelites saw Moses, his face was radiant, and they were afraid to come near him.**
>
> **But Moses called to them; so Aaron and all the leaders of the community came back to him, and he spoke to them.**

Afterward all the Israelites came near him, and he gave them all the commands the LORD had given him on Mount Sinai.

When Moses finished speaking to them, he put a veil over his face.

But whenever he entered the LORD's presence to speak with him, he removed the veil until he came out. And when he came out and told the Israelites what he had been commanded,

they saw that his face was radiant. Then Moses would put the veil back over his face until he went in to speak with the LORD.

Exodus 34:30-35

When you encounter God, it transforms you and the way you see the world and also the way others see you. Moses was so close to God it transformed his countenance so much that the people were afraid to come near him; His face was shining. What was it they were afraid of? I believe it was the reality of God, the awesome majestic presence of God. Many times in the Bible as people encountered God or the angels they would cry out in fear. There is something about God's reality that inspires this type of reaction.

Many of us ask why can't we see God? Why can't we experience Him? My response is: do we even try or give Him an opportunity to prove Himself? I am convinced if we allow Him to, He will prove His reality to us. God is real! In fact, He is more real than you are. You may think He is not real, but what you think doesn't change the fact that He is real and He is alive. He makes no apologies for who He is.

God is interested in you. He desires that no one should go through life without knowing Him. God will bend over backwards to prove Himself to you if you will only give Him a chance. I'm not talking about prayers like, "God if you do this, then I will believe." I'm talking about prayers like, "God if you are there and You exist I'm asking You to make yourself real to me." God will do that every time. He does not need me to defend Him. He does not need anyone to help Him out. He is more than capable of making Himself real to you if you will give Him a chance.

Throughout history and even in the present day, I believe those who claim to know God have misrepresented Him. I trust this book will go some way towards remedying this and take a step in the direction of settling the score of who God truly is. I don't want to be guilty of misrepresenting God to you. Let me share with you some thoughts about who I believe God is.

Chapter 3
Who is God?

God is beautiful. Words cannot describe how beautiful He is. How can we describe the indescribable? It is impossible. Is it possible that when we describe the living God to others, when we try to analyze Him, that we trivialize Him like some subject of discussion, like the News? Can we lose the sense of terrible beauty the living God inspires?

God is impossible to define in human terms: only some of our language can capture the smallest part of who He is and His indescribable beauty. I have a songwriter friend who said, of God "You are at once an enigma and then You're as plain as day. I will never claim to understand, but I wouldn't have it any other way."

Sometimes as God reveals Himself, men are frightened by the beauty and holiness of what they see.

[Isaiah said,] **"In the year that King Uzziah died, I saw the Lord seated on a throne, high and exalted, and the train of his robe filled the temple.**

Above him were seraphs, each with six wings: With two wings they covered their faces, with two they covered their feet, and with two they were flying.

And they were calling to one another: 'Holy, holy, holy is the LORD Almighty; the whole earth is full of his glory.'

At the sound of their voices the doorposts and thresholds shook and the temple was filled with smoke.

'Woe to me!' I cried. 'I am ruined! For I am a man of unclean lips, and I live among a people of unclean lips, and my eyes have seen the King, the LORD Almighty.'"

Isaiah 6:1-5

Isaiah saw something, which frightened him and caused him to cry out that he was a man undone. This was no ordinary encounter. This was something, which revolutionized him. When we truly meet with God, it will turn our life upside down.

The great revivalist Rodney Howard-Browne says, "when we have a cup of tea it is an experience. If we jump into a swimming pool we will have an experience. Don't tell me if you have an encounter with the living God you will not have an experience!" Something happens to us when we meet with God. God is more alive than we are. He is more real than we are. When we meet Him it is an incredible experience. We meet Life Himself. The very source of all life.

I remember being in India for an Evangelistic Campaign. While we were there, we spent some time with some gentlemen who were adherents to the Hindu religion. Wherever we go we make a point of respecting the religious faith of others, while presenting the truths of the Gospel. These gentlemen owned a hotel and we were in their business office talking with them. They expressed an interest in the Christian faith and were interested in what we were doing in ministry. We discussed the things of God together and we shared with them our experience of God. We discussed the claims of Christ and the need to have a real and vital relationship with God through Jesus Christ.

After a while it seemed like we had come to the end of our discussions, and nothing had happened which would open the door in their lives to a real relationship with God. They were both well educated, well informed and saw no need for any change. Because I sensed their continued interest and obvious spiritual hunger, I said to the two men, will you let me pray for you?

I began to pray for them and it seemed like a tremendous electric presence filled the room. After prayer I waited for a very long time; as these two men continued to sit with their eyes closed, they seemed to be experiencing something. After some time they opened their eyes and the older man said to me "all my life I feel like I have been a light bulb and I have been trying to flip the switch to turn the power on and nothing has happened. Now I feel like for the first time I have experienced the power I have been searching for."

What is this Power? What happened to these men? What was given to them in that moment? What was it that gave them the answer to their questions, to the things they had been searching for in their hearts? I believe it was the reality of the presence of God. I am convinced that nothing less than an experience with the tangible presence of God will convince some people of the existence of God or of the claims of Christianity. We need an encounter with the Living God!

God is deep and mysterious, beyond our human comprehension; to describe Him is like trying to describe the wind. He is beyond our wildest imaginations and beyond our wildest dreams. The Bible tells us in the book of Job that Job had an incredible encounter with God. Job knew God at a certain level. He had heard of God and tried his best to follow God and do everything right. He was a man who was faithful to God. God allowed him to be tested, terribly tested, because He had a greater purpose in mind.

God stripped Job of his family, his friends, and his business. Once Job had passed through his trial, God appeared to him in a great whirlwind. God's purpose with Job was to bring him closer. Job said "before my ears had heard of you and now my eyes have seen you." God challenged Job with the reality of His existence. God made no apology to Job for who He was. He showed up in his life and said, "this is who I am."

[God said to Job,] **"Where were you when I laid the earth's foundation? Tell me, if you understand,**

Who marked off its dimensions? Surely you know! Who stretched a measuring line across it?

On what were its footings set, or who laid its cornerstone while the morning stars sang together and all the angels shouted for joy?" **Job 38:4-7**

God was saying to Job that He was God and although Job was a righteous man who feared God and obeyed Him, he failed to understand the awesomeness, the reality and power of the living God.

Then Job replies to the Lord:

"I know that you can do all things; no plan of yours can be thwarted.

You asked, 'Who is this that obscures my counsel without knowledge?' Surely I spoke of things I did not understand, things too wonderful for me to know.

'You said, 'Listen now, and I will speak; I will question you, and you shall answer me.'

My ears had heard of you but now my eyes have seen you.

Therefore I despise myself and repent in dust and ashes."

Job 42:1-6

Job was truly awestruck with God. He had previously had a fairly good understanding of who God was. His religion had taught Him how to serve God and how to obey God, but there was something in this encounter, which changed Him forever. He was awestruck with the reality of God. He had heard of God, but when he actually saw God, when he actually met God it shook him to the core.

We can sit around and postulate about what we think God is like. We can agree or disagree as to whether we like things about His character and the way He does things, but when God turns up in our life all those thoughts quickly disappear. God is too awesome to describe; too beautiful for words and as human beings many times the only option left for us with an encounter like that is to apologize and say "sorry God I had no idea you were like that at all."

In the book of Acts we read in Chapter 1:3 that "After his suffering, he showed himself to these men and gave many convincing proofs that he was alive. He appeared to them over a period of forty days and spoke about the Kingdom of God." Jesus is willing to do whatever it takes to make sure we are aware of His existence. Convincing proofs, means that there was no doubt in anyone's mind that He was alive and risen from the dead.

After He arose from the dead, Jesus appeared to doubting Thomas. Thomas said "unless I see the nail prints in His hands and touch His side I will not believe." Many of us are like that. We can't believe unless we see something. God understands that sometimes we need to see something that leaves us with no doubt He exists.

God is truly compassionate and His compassion was shown in His willingness to come to Thomas and prove who He was. Jesus Christ came to all the doubters and He still comes to doubters today to prove the reality of His existence. He will come to you if you are willing to let Him.

Before he became a Christian, the Apostle Paul was a persecutor of the Christian faith named Saul. He persecuted and killed Christians. As he was riding his horse on his way to do more harm to believers, he had a powerful encounter with the risen Jesus Christ. A great light shone upon him from heaven. He was knocked from his horse and Jesus spoke to him and said, "Why are you persecuting me?" Jesus defended Himself. He was having no more of the persecution of His people. In the process of defending Himself, Jesus revealed Himself in all His glory to Saul. He wanted Saul to know that He was intimately involved with His people, but also that He was very much alive.

As Paul grew as a Christian his encounters with God continued. He had encounters with God which were indescribable. The Bible tells us that Paul was "was caught up to paradise. He heard inexpressible things, things that man is not permitted to tell" (2 Corinthians 12:4). Paul knew that when you encounter heaven and God Himself, the things you see are completely indescribable, unspeakable.

God delights in revealing His unspeakable nature to His children. Every one of us was born with an innate longing and desire for these beautiful unspeakable things. It is in our make-up to desire the things of heaven. Each of us is like a child without a home, without a father. When we meet with God we meet the God of the universe, the God of the impossible.

We wonder sometimes where God is but when His moment is right, He has the ability to defend Himself, to reveal to us who He is. God does not need me to defend His reality. He will defend Himself. He will stand up for Himself. He will make Himself real to you.

The great prophet Moses could not look upon the face of God and live, God's face was just all too powerful and terrible to behold (Exodus 33:23). God makes no excuses for who He is. He is God and He will not be conformed to what we would like Him to be. If God is who He says He is and He is real then I am believing He will make Himself real to you. That He will satisfy the hunger in your soul for Him. God wants to do that for you.

Chapter 4
God is Looking for Real People

I remember as a child and as a young person, never really being satisfied with the claims of Christianity. I was always skeptical. I was always questioning the fundamental beliefs and assertions of Christianity. In my heart I wanted to believe, but what I was presented with did not satisfy the longing I had to really meet God. I felt church was irrelevant and that the Christian faith was full of holes and ambiguity.

The church and the believers of the first Century were people who could not be ignored. Like us, they lived in a pluralistic hedonistic culture, which had many and varying beliefs about life and the Universe and yet they had something happening in their lives which impacted the culture of the day fundamentally.

The Church had a power and reality of God present, which could not be ignored, could not be sidelined or silenced. This is what is desperately needed today. Christianity today has become a religion devoid of spiritual reality in some sectors and in need of radical overhaul. It needs revival. It needs to have the kind of supernatural power and reality, which cannot be ignored by society.

People in society should sit up and listen when the church has something to say, but right now, the church is considered by many to be irrelevant to the modern world. It is seen as a historic institution, which has lost touch with the real world, a relic of an earlier stage of civilization. People in many places now scorn Christians. They have become socially marginalized and are considered by many to be strange people, people who "hear voices."

Our society is skeptical of God and the supernatural. There is more than intellectual persuasion required to convince people of God's reality. The youth and all segments of society need to see that God is real. The Christian faith needs to persuade people God is real and the only way it can be persuasive is if God's people are real, and they have a real relationship with God.

What does it mean to be real? It means to be honest about what we feel and think. If we are real with God, God will be real with us. I used to pray a prayer before I was a Christian that went something like "God if you are out there and you can prove to me beyond a shadow of doubt that you exist then I will believe."

God saw my heart and my willingness to be real with Him. I was not interested in religion. I wanted the real thing or nothing. I want to encourage you to be real with God whether or not you are a Christian. Begin to pray prayers that are more like a conversation with your best friend. Open up your heart and be real.

People in our society are looking for real people. They can spot a fake a mile away. I'm trusting as you read this book you can sense some genuineness, some realness. I'm trusting you will feel that this book is something you can relate to because it is real. If you are satisfied that what is in this book is real, then I want to encourage you to be real with God. God will make

Himself real to you. He did it for me, He can do it for you. Why not?

You don't have to be perfect for God to reveal Himself to you. There is something that happens when we are real with God. Don't kid yourself, God knows what you are thinking anyway, so you might as well be up front and share what's on your mind. I remember one time sharing about the reality of God with a young man, who wasn't a Christian. He said "I don't believe in God." I shared with him as I had with many others and said "you know it really doesn't matter what you believe, if God is real He will prove it to you."

We in our arrogance and pride say, "I don't believe in God." Did you ever stop to think for a moment about what would happen if God decided He didn't believe in you? The Bible tells us God holds all things together by the Word of His power. If God decided that you didn't exist or He didn't believe in you, you would be turned into a million pieces of cosmic dust in a heartbeat. I'm not trying to belittle you, but I believe God is real and if He decided that you weren't real for some reason then your life would be over.

The bottom line is that God is real! He doesn't need anyone's help to prove that. Every person is different. You may have different objections to God. You may have different needs. You may take less convincing to believe than others, you may need to be convinced of the authenticity of Scripture, you may need to be convinced of the existence of a Creator, you may need a direct encounter with God in order to believe.

It is not a sin to ask God to demonstrate His reality to you. God knows where you are at today. Maybe you are concerned about some of the claims of Christianity.

29

Maybe you aren't happy with what you perceive are things about God which are unjust.

Many people feel that all of the suffering in this world should not be allowed by a loving God. Some people believe that God is unjust sending people to hell forever. Some feel that evolution and science is the answer to creation or the existence of God. Some feel that God is out there somewhere, it's just that they haven't met Him yet.

It seems there is always some reason, some excuse for not believing in the reality of God or the claims of Christianity. God knows where you are at with Him, but I want to challenge you, whether you believe it or not *God is real*. Be real with God and tell Him your objections. Ask Him to make Himself real to you.

Maybe you are thinking, "I have never considered God or His reality; my life is too busy focusing on just getting on with life. I am too busy to consider whether God is real; these are the deep issues of life and I don't have time to think about things like that."

It is my belief that even if you are not looking for God or not interested in Him at all, there is still something on the inside, which you are trying to cover up with your busyness, or with your party lifestyle. Everyone is made in God's image and have an innate need for relationship with God whether they like it or not.

Recently I was at home in New Zealand, in a Starbucks coffee shop reading my Bible and a lady saw me there. We got to talking and I could see a hunger inside of her heart. We talked about God and His reality. She proceeded to tell me all the many and varied reasons why she didn't believe in God or Christianity.

She was a very intelligent person, and had a complex set of reasons why she did not believe, but even while I sat there listening to her I could see her looking over at my Bible with hunger in her eyes. Even though she denied Christianity, her belief system was robbing her of having that spiritual hunger satisfied. You see it doesn't matter which way you dice it, God created human beings for relationship with Him and you can argue all you want — the reality is there is a hunger inside of you that can only be satisfied when you meet with God and have a relationship with Him.

That lady had something in her which was undeniable. I listened to her multiple and varied arguments about why God did not exist or why Christianity was not the true religion. It didn't matter what she believed in her head, there was still a hunger within her, which she couldn't hide. It is incomprehensively sad that we live in a world, which due to the beliefs and philosophies of our time make it very difficult for people to develop a real, lasting and meaningful relationship with God.

Maybe you are like I was; you want to believe God is there, but you need something to happen to prove to you He is real. God will do that for you. Maybe like many people in this life, you have a mixture of different beliefs about life. You believe "to each his own, or that might be good for you, but that's not my thing — whatever makes you happy." This kind of relativism is common in western society.

I believe relativism is our excuse for not facing the truth, the absolute truth. If we say God is real, then He must be the God who created all of us. His laws and principles also apply to each of us in the same way. When you meet God you will understand that there is an absolute truth, an absolute norm and a system of values, which is determined by God. We are all accountable to God for all of our actions and decisions.

31

Maybe you don't believe in sin, or heaven or hell or anything which represents accountability for your actions. Maybe you are happy just the way you are. Maybe you have nothing you are concerned about at all, maybe you have everything you need in life and you are happy, and you don't need any help from God.

My response to you is that if you can only get introduced to God everything will change. Meeting with God is the most incredible breathtaking experience you will ever have. You think everything is great right now, but meeting God is that much greater. There is a deeper and more meaningful reality to life for you to experience, a richness of satisfaction that only an encounter with God can bring.

Jesus demonstrated this to us when He came to Earth. In Jesus' earthly ministry, he shared the truths concerning His mission with a Samaritan woman. She had been trying to find satisfaction in relationships. She had had many husbands and the man she was living with was not her husband. Jesus began to speak to her about drinking living water, which would give her the true satisfaction she was looking for.

We read this account in John 4:5-30; 39-42:

So he [Jesus] came to a town in Samaria called Sychar, near the plot of ground Jacob had given to his son Joseph.

Jacob's well was there, and Jesus, tired as he was from the journey, sat down by the well. It was about the sixth hour.

When a Samaritan woman came to draw water, Jesus said to her,

"Will you give me a drink?"

(His disciples had gone into the town to buy food.)

The Samaritan woman said to him, "You are a Jew and I am a Samaritan woman. How can you ask me for a drink?" (For Jews do not associate with Samaritans.)

Jesus answered her, "If you knew the gift of God and who it is that asks you for a drink, you would have asked him and he would have given you living water."

"Sir," the woman said, "you have nothing to draw with and the well is deep. Where can you get this living water?

Are you greater than our father Jacob, who gave us the well and drank from it himself, as did also his sons and his flocks and herds?"

Jesus answered, "Everyone who drinks this water will be thirsty again,

but whoever drinks the water I give him will never thirst. Indeed, the water I give him will become in him a spring of water welling up to eternal life."

The woman said to him, "Sir, give me this water so that I won't get thirsty and have to keep coming here to draw water."

He told her, "Go, call your husband and come back."

"I have no husband," she replied. Jesus said to her, "You are right when you say you have no husband.

The fact is, you have had five husbands, and the man you now have is not your husband. What you have just said is quite true."

"Sir," the woman said, "I can see that you are a prophet.

Our fathers worshiped on this mountain, but you Jews claim that the place where we must worship is in Jerusalem."

Jesus declared, "Believe me, woman, a time is coming when you will worship the Father neither on this mountain nor in Jerusalem.

You Samaritans worship what you do not know; we worship what we do know, for salvation is from the Jews.

Yet a time is coming and has now come when the true worshipers will worship the Father in spirit and truth, for they are the kind of worshipers the Father seeks.

God is spirit, and his worshipers must worship in spirit and in truth."

The woman said, "I know that Messiah (called Christ) is coming. When he comes, he will explain everything to us."

Then Jesus declared, "I who speak to you am he."

Just then his disciples returned and were surprised to find him talking with a woman. But no one asked, "What do you want?" or "Why are you talking with her?"

Then, leaving her water jar, the woman went back to the town and said to the people,

"Come, see a man who told me everything I ever did. Could this be the Christ?"

They came out of the town and made their way toward him.

Many of the Samaritans from that town believed in him because of the woman's testimony, "He told me everything I ever did."

So when the Samaritans came to him, they urged him to stay with them, and he stayed two days.

And because of his words many more became believers.

They said to the woman, "We no longer believe just because of what you said; now we have heard for ourselves, and we know that this man really is the Savior of the world."

In this story we see Jesus did a number of things. It's one of the great evangelistic passages of Scripture in the Bible. Jesus demonstrates a supernatural knowledge of the woman's life which convinces her of His legitimacy and it opens up everyone in the village to the reality of Jesus and his mission.

Jesus said, "I will give you something which will satisfy your thirst. My presence, my reality will fulfill your deepest longings and your deepest needs." There is a beauty in relationship with God which can change you and fulfill you and satisfy you like nothing else.

Maybe like this woman, you feel like you have everything you need, you have no need of anything else, but there is something inside you which can only be satisfied with God. When you taste that living water, you will find the satisfaction you need. It is when you come to understand the possibility that God is real and He is supernatural, that you can see that your need is greater than you realize.

Before we encounter God it is like we are immune, we have a lack of sensitivity to the reality of God. We actually believe we are happy, we have everything we need. Sometimes it takes a supernatural encounter with God to show us our need; we actually need God's help to show us we have need of Him. It is like we are in a dream world, a world which we believe is real and we need God to wake us up, in order to see things the way they really are.

Maybe you say well, I already have a system of faith, I have another religion that is not Christianity and I have found the satisfaction and the answers I need for life in that religion. I want to challenge you to consider the issues I address in the seventh chapter of this book. I want you to consider the possibility that a vital two way relationship with the Living God is something God wants for you. Many religions teach us the way to God and how we can become better people, but typically they do not help us to encounter God and have a relationship with God.

Maybe you are living a certain lifestyle and you feel that if you encounter God everything will change and you will be forced to let go of some things you like doing, to make some lifestyle changes. The heart is an interesting thing. We want to do what is in our heart. When your heart changes, your desires change. When you meet God and He steals your heart away, everything will change.

Maybe you say well, I believe this world came into being through the Big Bang theory and the theory of evolution. I don't believe in Christianity's notion of a Creator God. Christians believe God is a supernatural God. The Bible tells us He is invisible and that He is Spirit, heaven is His throne and earth is His footstool.

It tells us He spoke the material and the spiritual world into existence. God said "Let there be" and it was. God is more real than His creation. As His creatures we like to insist that God does not exist, but deep within the human heart is that knowing. We can try and cover over it and submerge it and harden our hearts against it, but it is always there.

The Bible tells us creation speaks of the existence of God. The world has been designed by an Intelligent Designer. Creation has a message in and of itself that God is real. It cries out "there is a God!" Someone once said it is harder to prove that God does not exist than to prove that He does exist. I believe that anyone who is intellectually honest would have a difficult time arguing for God's non-existence.

I remember years ago picking up some hitchhikers and the one in the front seat was telling me about the Big Bang theory and the theory of evolution. I said to him "creation is so complex, it is almost impossible to deny that there was an Intelligent Designer who created all things."

The hitchhiker in the back seat was a tourist from the United Kingdom who was working on his Phd. in Physics. He said the people he studied with were now convinced that the Big Bang theory and the theory of evolution were statistically an impossibility. The odds against them occurring were so high that they were written off as an impossibility.

I laughed and said to the guy in the front seat "there goes your theories, from the mouths of the scientists, not me." He was a little bit troubled and then went on to tell me about the spaceman theory. This is the theory that at some point in history all the earth was visited by spacemen who set things up in order for intelligent life to exist.

In all honesty at this point I was somewhat frustrated. This guy wasn't interested in proving the truths of the theory of evolution or the Big Bang theory, he just wanted, something, anything to avoid considering the possibility that there was a Creator. I believe deep down he knew God was there, but He didn't want to even have to consider that possibility. It would mean that he would have to be accountable to someone for the actions of his life.

This may be where you are at as you read this book. You may be looking everywhere other than God because you don't want to be accountable to Him for your life. Let me encourage you that God isn't so bad, not only is He not so bad, He's awesome, He's indescribable. I want to challenge you to stop running from God and tell God you are willing to meet with Him if He is willing to meet with you. I know God will honor that prayer.

Society now is filled with unbelief. I want to argue that what you believe is many times determined by the society in which you live; what you have been taught by your family or your society. Your reality is determined by what you have been taught. Many times what society tells us is not the truth, it is commonly held error. Our reality is not based on truth.

Chapter 5
What is Reality?

I want to give some of the background to the development of the broader ideology influencing society today so we can try to understand what framework we are working with and how it is we understand reality. In much of western society, and in communist countries, reality is seen as something which we perceive with our senses or that we know from experience.

Reality is seen as something which does not include God or the supernatural. Our perennial slogan is "if you can't see it, then it cannot exist." God cannot be seen or proved empirically, therefore God does not exist. This is the mindset pervading much of secular society today. This has become how we view reality.

Secularism is the widely held value system of many in today's western world. It has become the way in which we understand the world. Typically, secularism includes an anti-religious, anti-God philosophy. It is composed of people who are atheistic or agnostic or those who are simply ignostic, having no concept of God or Christianity and who hold no view on religious matters.[3]

Secularism has become an institution in many parts of the western world, in countries, which were the heart of old Christendom. The countries which fall into this category are: "Great Britain, Europe, Scandinavia, Canada, Australia and New Zealand."[4]

There are a number of differing types of secularism: (a) Utter secularity: promoted by Voltaire and Marx and found in countries such as France and communist countries. (b) Mere secularity: the church is ignored and considered irrelevant, however the culture still has a sense of its Christian heritage. This is found in countries such as Great Britain. (c) Controlled secularity: Christianity is widespread and secularism is vying for dominance. This is found in countries such as the United States.

Secular society holds the view that supernaturalism is "the vestigial notion of some less developed stage of humanity's evolution."[6] Time is understood in terms of billions of years, and the future seems to stretch out in an endless stretch of time. The basis for understanding the origins of life is scientific and rational, and anything outside of these parameters is considered irrational.

In secular society people typically do not have any beliefs regarding salvation or anything remotely religious or Christian. Many in secular society have no conception of the message of Christianity, and typically if they do, they reject the message as irrelevant.[7] Christians are viewed as narrow minded and dogmatic, and unable to understand the complexities of life.[8]

Because the ideology of secularism predominates many western societies, it has control of much of mainstream thought which includes the media, and the sciences. Christian views which contradict the secular world-view are perceived as abnormal.

In our secular world, people are more concerned with the present life than with life after death. The enjoyment of life has now become the overwhelming obsession. This type of culture is prevalent in Australia and New Zealand to the point that these countries are now perceived as being the most hedonistic societies in the western world.[9]

Because of the factors detailed, secular people are not concerned with guilt any more, rather their concern is with doubt.[10] Christianity has appealed to secular peo-

40

ple on the basis of their sinfulness and the need of a Savior. It is my belief that the emphasis needs to be on helping people to come to a place where they can encounter God supernaturally. This is the emphasis of this book. I have written this book for secular people, who are struggling with doubt. If that's you, I have written this book for you.

There are many people in secular society who want to consider the possibility of God, but their whole life they have understood reality in concrete, measurable terms. For this reason the concept of the supernatural is foreign to them. They have a real struggle with the concept that God exists. Maybe that is you. You are having a real struggle with the issues I have raised in this book, and yet in spite of your doubts, you want to believe, but you can't.

We live in a doubting Thomas society or generation and I believe it is a tangible encounter with God which will convince you of the claims of Christianity and the existence of God. It is my job to show you if nothing else, that it is possible for you to encounter God.

Secularism has its roots in the atheistic world-view. Atheism has influenced the development of secular society, but society has not always been secular. It has not always been influenced by atheism. Many of the great thinkers and scientists and philosophers of history believed there was a supernatural God and their theories sought to understand and prove God's existence.

Descartes was a Christian who sought to prove the existence of God. He taught that everything was open to doubt except conscious experience and that existence was a necessary condition of conscious experience. "I think, therefore I am." From this premise he argued for the existence of God.

41

In society today, atheists have used the very same arguments and the logical conclusion for them of this premise is that the only truth there is, is found in the subjective consciousness and historicity of the human being. No truth or concept of reality can be found outside these parameters. Atheistic arguments reject the possibility of a transcendent realm or a transcendent truth.

Historically, this atheistic view of reality began to pervade society when people began to challenge the prevalent biblical world-view. Atheism, a word which may have at one time brought scorn and attached stigma in society, has now become culturally acceptable in most parts of the world. Atheism has a rich, colorful and at the same time arguably infamous history. The impact of it's thought on contemporary society has been far reaching.

Many western societies have become secularized by its influence. Many eastern societies have been transformed by atheistic communist regimes. During the two centuries following the reformation (1520-1780), atheism as a belief system was illegal.[11] The word *atheism* entered the vocabulary of society soon after the reformation, but it was not until the late eighteenth century that the first systematic defenses of unbelief appeared in print.[12]

In France, the learned culture of the day took it for granted that atheism was a moral, and not a philosophical phenomenon. They viewed those who did not believe as being similar to the fool of Psalm 14. They also believed that society was not able to function in an orderly manner without faith in God.[13]

It was during this period with missionary endeavors to many, particularly eastern cultures, that reports began to come back of highly developed non-Christian societies. This had the effect of shattering the prevailing

Christian world-view and led to many questioning the validity of the foundations of this world-view.[14]

The prevalent Christian world-view was considered philosophically and scientifically justifiable. Once this view was challenged, the Church left the defense of the faith to philosophers and scientists. "It was then a short step for the French materialists to combine Descartes mathematical nature, Newton's science, and a vitalistic biology to create a system that explained everything without any supernatural Deity and that explained the Judeo-Christian world as a natural development within the human world."[15]

Atheism has now spread to many parts of the world. In the East, atheism is organized, politicized; its leaders hold the reigns of political, economic and spiritual power. While many communist regimes have now collapsed, atheism is still virulent world-wide and in the Western world where Christianity was once virulent; a bland form of atheism has now become prevalent.[16]

Atheism arises from a mentality and attitude which involves a flight from the invisible towards the visible; from the transcendent towards the immanent; from the spiritual toward the material in such a way that not only are the invisible, transcendent and spiritual rejected as dimensions of reality, but they are denied existence itself.[17]

Atheism is not a merely speculative system aimed at proving in a rational manner that the existence of God is neither actual nor possible. Modern atheists are not atheists because they are incapable of finding and using the means to encounter God. Their denial of God is their choice of a crusade against God and their refusal to submit to any Being who would hold them accountable for their actions.[18]

Although the atheist may seem perfectly happy with their world-view, the reality is, every person is made in the image of God, and created for relationship with God. If the atheist was to be completely honest, feelings of the possibility that God is real would haunt them from time to time. Maybe you are atheist reading this book, And you have experienced those moments where, like C.S. Lewis, you sense the unrelenting approach of the Creator.

I believe there is no way to run from God, nowhere to hide. He is constantly in pursuit of all of His children. It is my belief that the atheist is reacting to something. They are in a fight against God. God is always trying to prove His reality and the atheist is always trying to put up philosophical and scientific defenses against Him.

They attack everything God is and everything God stands for, but God will not be denied. He is always knocking at the door of the human heart searching and longing, watching and waiting for every unbeliever to open their heart and let Him in.

In our minds, reality is something which we think is set in stone, but in fact, God is the supreme or ultimate reality. What God says goes! His reality is more real than ours. We have created a reality which excludes Him, but the ultimate reality is God's reality.

Chapter 6
Signs that Point Us
To the Reality of God

B ecause we as human beings are finite and God is infinite, it is impossible for us to fully know God. God has however done so much to reveal Himself to us. God reveals Himself to us through general and special revelation.

General revelation involves God revealing Himself through three means: nature, history and the constitution of the human being, and special revelation is the written record of His interaction with humanity.[19]

The very world and universe is our starting point for understanding how God reveals Himself to us. The scripture states in Romans 1:20 that, "For since the creation of the world God's invisible qualities — his eternal power and divine nature — have been clearly seen, being understood from what has been made, so that men are without excuse." There are other scriptures which clearly indicate that God reveals Himself to humanity through nature or His creation.

Every time we look at the stars in the sky and the beauty of nature, we are reminded that God is real. God intended for these things to speak to us and remind us that He is the Creator of them all. Maybe you have looked at all these things and wondered "Is God out there somewhere?" This is God speaking to you, causing you to wonder if He is there. He is revealing Himself to you through Creation.

There is a new school of thought which challenges the assumptions of evolution and the Big Bang theory. It is the called the Theory of Intelligent Design. This theory began in the latter half of the 20th Century and its aim is to promote an even deeper investigation of nature to uncover every aspect of its complexity. It is the assertion that certain features of the universe and of living things are best explained by an Intelligent Cause, not an undirected process such as natural selection.

Evolution and some of the other theories promulgated concerning the origins of life and the universe assume that the earth is the product of time and change and the evolution of the species, through the process of natural selection. I always used to wonder and still do if scientists believe the world began with a big bang and time and chance happened to them, where did the big bang come from? Where did the elements comprising the big bang come from? In order for an explosion to happen there must have been some matter present, some elements to combust.

The theories and origins of life promoted by the scientific community do not leave us with a rock solid sense of security that life began as they suggest. These theories in my opinion require an element of faith, it seems to me that science has almost become a belief system with an agenda to deny God's existence.

The basic premise of the Theory of Intelligent Design is that in our world and in our universe there is much evidence for the existence of an Intelligent Designer. To use a crude analogy, if we consider a park bench and its simple design, it is built with the purpose of having someone sit on it, enjoy the view, and rest their legs. The bench is designed with a purpose in mind and required a measure of intelligence to design it. It must have had an intelligent designer.

When we consider human beings and the complexity of how they function, how much more intelligence is required to design such complexity? Human beings were designed by God for the purpose of a relationship with Him, and there is tremendous evidence purely due to the complexity of design for an Intelligent Designer.

Another illustration I like to use is, if we take one ton of scrap metal and leave it in a garage, what will be there when we open the door of the garage in one year? A pile of scrap metal of course. Now if we open the door in 100 years we will get the same result. If we open the door in one million years, the result will also be the same, although the metal will probably have rusted into dust. Science would have us believe that if we open the door in one million years we would find a Mercedes Benz sitting in the garage.

This analogy can be stretched further. Science would have us believe that the metal developed into an amoeba, and an amoeba developed into a number of different species of animal and eventually we open the garage door and an elephant is standing there.

Science attempts to convince all of us that anything is possible over millions of years. There is a measure of faith required. Well, I don't buy it. I don't buy that everything we see is the product of random acts occurring over the millennia. There is too much order, there is too much intricate design and interdependency required for advanced life forms to exist.

Due to the almost impossibility and inconceivability of the randomness of the theory of evolution, and other theories of the origins of the Universe, many scientists now adhere to the Anthropic principle. The principle argues that all the forces and laws of nature are set in place in order to allow advanced life forms to exist.

The force of gravity, the electromagnetic force constant, the size of the strong and the weak nuclear force are finely tuned to allow for galaxies, stars, planets, atmospheres and living systems to be self sustained by those laws. If any of these forces were slightly greater or less in force, then advanced life could not exist.

Whether or not we agree with Intelligent Design as being a valid scientific theory, it does point to some incredible co-incidences, which if drawn to their logical conclusion become impossibilities if we don't consider the possibility of a Creator or Intelligent Designer.

In short, God made it almost impossible for the intellectually honest human being to come to the conclusion that He didn't create everything. God reveals Himself to you through His Creation. It is an act of His love for you, He's pointing you in His direction, and He is waiting for you to respond to His promptings, His nudging.

God reveals Himself through the human constitution. God has made humans in His own image. Humans have the ability to make moral judgments. Paul states in Romans 2:11-16 that God has written a law on the hearts of persons who do not have the specially revealed law. Every society has a code of behavior which reflects the innate knowing that every human being has, that there are some things which are right and some things which are wrong.

Maybe you have wondered about this, how it is that within all human beings there is an innate knowing of what is right and what is wrong. Psychology and Sociology argue that all behaviors are learned, but I don't agree. Somehow God has hard-wired into every human being an instinctive and innate knowing of right and wrong. Many call this the conscience. I believe the conscience is warning us that to live a certain way in violation of God's principles can be damaging to us and to others.

Maybe there have been moments in your life and you have wondered, "how did I just know that? No one told me, I just knew it was wrong." This is conscience speaking to you, ultimately it is God speaking to you and pointing you in His direction.

Humanity has a religious instinct, a desire to worship. Every person whether secular or religious has this desire, whether it be bowing down to an idol, or following a theory or philosophy. Some people worship material things. Every tribal group that has been discovered throughout history has a series of beings they worship and has developed a complex set of rituals they observe. This desire to worship came from the Creator and points to God as the object of human desire.

I said earlier, that not being able to meet with God is like a child having no opportunity to meet with his/her parents. Every child has an instinctive need for love and for their parents. Studies show a child deprived of the love of parents in the formative years has serious developmental deficiencies. Each child has certain needs. Instinctively, and even without anyone telling them, humans have the need to worship to have relationship with God.

Many communist nations have tried to suppress this need, to pretend it does not exist; but all they have succeeded in doing is creating an environment for an even more fervent breed of Christianity. Those who believe, know they face possible persecution, but they must have this need for relationship with God satisfied. Many have been prepared to die for their faith rather than forsake it. They love God more than life.

Let me say at this point the issue of martyrdom has been something which has baffled those rulers and regimes throughout history who have been determined to crush Christianity. They have been shocked to see how deep and how important relationship with God is to those who know Him. Martyrdom is something which has typically been a Christian phenomenon historically.

There are so many powerful stories I could share concerning this issue, but let me share a couple with you, which I believe so poignantly illustrate the depth of human commitment to relationship with God. In sharing this I am trying to give you some idea of how much of an impact God can make on a human life. It seems that life itself becomes less important to some people than what God means to them.

Perpertua (203 ad) was a North African Christian who was martyred under the reign of Emperor Septimus Severus. Perpetua stood firm in her decision after her imprisonment, despite having a new born baby and an aged father who pleaded with her to gain her freedom by denying Christ. She was tossed and gored by an infuriated bull in the amphitheater, fell into a trance and was unaware of any pain. Finally a gladiator came forward and cut off her head, after stabbings with a sword failed to kill her.

Martina (226 ad) was a woman of Roman nobility. She was burned at the stake for her faith, but came out uninjured. Emperor Severus ordered her head cut off thinking she was a magician with power in her hair.

Taken to the temple of Diana, part of the building burned down when she made the sign of the cross. She was then taken to the amphitheater, where a lion was let loose upon her and became tame when it drew near. The lion then turned and attacked Eumenus, the emperor's father, who had influenced his son to persecute Christians. The lion tore Eumenus to pieces.

In the end, Martina was taken to the temple of Apollo. At the sign of the cross, Apollo's image fell and was broken to pieces. The ground shook and part of the building fell upon the temple priests and the worshippers. Four torturers were sent to kill Martina, but angels intervened. Eight more were sent, but a force stopped them from hurting Martina. They immediately converted to Christ. At this point the emperor ordered that all of them had their heads cut off. Martina's suffering was over.[20]

How do we explain such radical and seemingly fanatical commitment to something to the point people have been willing to die for it. Many of us have philosophies and religions we believe in, but how many of us would be willing to die for these philosophies?

There is something deep and powerful at work here. It is my opinion, these stories point us to the love of God and the reality of God. No one gives their life up for nothing. These people had a certainty that there was a God who could be related to. They were willing to give up all that was precious to them in order to keep that relationship.

In addition to all the other ways God reveals Himself, He has revealed Himself in special terms. God's special revelation is "God's manifestation of Himself to particular persons at definite times and places, enabling those persons to enter into a redemptive relationship with Him."[21] God has revealed Himself in a Holy Land to a Holy People and this revelation was recorded in a Holy Book, the Holy Bible. The Bible reveals to us the nature of God, His actions in creation, the fall of humanity and the redemption of humanity. There are more specific details about God and the way He operates in the Bible.

The Bible contains many references as to how it was formulated.

All scripture is God breathed [inspired]....
2 Timothy 3:16

For prophecy never had its origin in the will of man, but men spoke from God as they were carried along by the Holy Spirit. **2 Peter 1:21**

Archaeology confirms the validity and historicity of Scripture. Archaeologist Joseph Free said that "Archaeology has confirmed countless passages which had been rejected by critics as unhistorical or contrary to known facts."[22] Renowned Jewish archaeologist Nelson Gluek confidently said that "It...may be stated categorically that no archaeological discovery has ever controverted a biblical reference. Scores of archeological findings have been made which confirm in clear outline or exact detail historical statements in the Bible."[23]

For the New Testament, Dr. G.R. Habermas points out that within 110 years of Christ's crucifixion, approximately eighteen non-Christian sources mention more than "one hundred facts, beliefs, and teachings from the life of Christ and early Christendom. These items, I might add, mention almost every major detail of Jesus' life, including miracles, the Resurrection, and His claims to deity."[24]

Sir Frederick Kenyon, who was second to none in issuing statements about manuscripts, said this about the New Testament: "The interval between the dates of original composition and the earliest existing evidence (i.e. the earliest copies we have) become so small to be in fact negligible, and the last foundation for any doubt that the Scriptures have come down to us substantially as having been written has now been removed. Both the authenticity and general integrity of the New Testament may be regarded as finally established."[25] He also said that "No fundamental doctrine of the Christian faith rests on a disputed reading."[26]

When considering special revelation and other forms of written revelation, many have trouble with deciding which faith is the true faith. They think "after all doesn't every form of faith have its own holy book?" Sometimes it is God Himself who must show up in their situation to prove He is the True God. To show that Christianity is the true faith, God needs to do a miracle.

Chapter 7
The Fire of God and the Reality of God

Well, where do I begin? I could try to say many things to impress you and to try and convince you of God's existence. There are things I could tell you to try and convince you that Jesus is the only way to God, but I know you are tired of empty words, empty speeches and empty books. There is a hunger within each human heart for something real, something supernatural, something of God which is tangible.

There is much done in the name of the religions of the world, which ultimately hinders people from experiencing the power and reality of the living God. Religion may provide us with a way to live life, but very little of the reality of God. There are millions of people in this world, who are in the grip of secularism and who do not even believe in God. Why? They have seen a form of religion, but they do not see any power to back it up.

There are many who adhere to the different religious beliefs of this world. They have been taught a system of belief that will lead them to God or a state of bliss. They believe that if they lead good lives they will please God. Even with all their religion offers, they are left without a meaningful relationship with their Creator.

It is my firm conviction that nothing less than the demonstration of God's power will sway some people. Nothing less will satisfy their hunger for the reality of God. Many times, it is a demonstration of the miracle power of God and the fire of God which settles the issue of who the true God is.

Jesus said, "I am the Way the truth and the life, no-one comes to the Father but by me" (John 14:6). When we meet Jesus we find the way to God and God is willing to do anything and everything to demonstrate this truth. In the course of history, God has done this very thing. He has worked to demonstrate to those who do not truly know him, to those who were subject to fallible ideologies, philosophies and religious beliefs and practices.

In First Kings 18:21-24 God spoke to a Prophet. God used this Prophet to demonstrate to the people of his generation that He was the true and living God. The people of Elijah's generation worshipped the gods of Baal and Asherah. God spoke to Elijah and set things up to demonstrate to the people that there was only one God.

Elijah was the last prophet left in all the land of Israel. All the other prophets of God had been slaughtered by those who adhered to the other religions of the day. The people had no fear of God and no faith in God. The Bible says, "Do not touch my anointed ones; do my prophets no harm" (1 Chronicles 16:22), but these people had no fear of God and had totally dishonored Him.

It was time for God to show them that He was real. God came as a mighty fire to demonstrate His reality. There are many religions, many philosophies, many things we can believe in, but there is only one God who answers by fire. There is one God, who is real, and this is what God was trying to show the people. The issue of which religion is the true religion, and which God is the true God needed to be settled.

We read that the great prophet Elijah called all the people of Israel together and He said:

> **Then Elijah said to them, "I am the only one of the LORD's prophets left, but Baal has four hundred and fifty prophets.**
>
> **Get two bulls for us. Let them choose one for themselves, and let them cut it into pieces and put it on the wood but not set fire to it. I will prepare the other bull and put it on the wood but not set fire to it.**
>
> **Then you call on the name of your god, and I will call on the name of the LORD. The god who answers by fire — he is God." Then all the people said, "What you say is good."**
>
> **1 Kings 18:22-24**

All day the prophets of Baal called out to their gods and had no response. In 1 Kings 18:37-40 we read what happened as Elijah prayed:

> **"Answer me, O LORD, answer me, so these people will know that you, O LORD, are God, and that you are turning their hearts back again."**
>
> **Then the fire of the LORD fell and burned up the sacrifice, the wood, the stones and the soil, and also licked up the water in the trench.**
>
> **When all the people saw this, they fell prostrate and cried, 'The LORD — He is God! The LORD — He is God!"**

It is worth noting that the fire which fell from heaven was no ordinary fire. It was a supernatural fire. It was God's way of proving His reality to all who were present. God is pure and holy, His fire cleanses and purges sin and all forms of evil. The fire was the Holy

Spirit; the Bible tells us God is a consuming fire (Deuteronomy 4:24).

The Bible tells us that when the Holy Spirit fell at the commencement of the Church, He fell as a consuming fire (Acts 2). Fire is something which catches, it cannot easily be controlled, and when God comes as fire He changes everything. Earthly fire can be both beneficial and destructive. When God comes like fire He destroys sin and evil and builds godliness, holiness and righteousness into the lives of His people.

All the people in the land were following their respective religions; they were walking in darkness and it took one man's obedience to change the situation. Sometimes all it takes is one person to stand up and say God is real. God will back you up if you are willing to do that. Elijah asked God what shall I do about this problem? It was all part of God's plan. God wanted the people to know the right way to Him.

As I write this book, I am building an altar to God by faith. I believe His fire will fall from heaven on your life and God will do something supernatural to prove to you that He exists. Like Elijah, there are times when we cry out to God and say I am the only one left following You in this godforsaken place.

I need You to show up. I need you to show these people You are real. I need you to do something supernatural. Like Elijah when we obey, sometimes God has to show up, to glorify His Name. When God's Name and honor are at stake, if we work in partnership with Him, He will show up. I am believing that as I write this book in obedience to God, He will send His fire and do the impossible to prove to you that He exists.

Sometimes the circumstances look hopeless, no one else is willing to obey or follow Jesus. When God's fire begins to fall everything changes in an instant. When people see the reality of God everything changes. This is what happened to me and it can happen to you.

There are not many Christians in some parts of this world, and it may look like God is not active. I don't care how impossible things look right now. I don't care if you don't believe what I am telling you. God has called me to share these things with you, and even if nothing happens and I stand here with egg on my face, I will have done what God told me to do. Something happened with Elijah, and I believe something will happen in your life.

I want to challenge you the way Elijah challenged the people of Israel. How long will you falter between two opinions? If God be God then serve Him, if other gods be god then serve them. As Jesus Christ proves Himself real to you, I want to challenge you to forsake all others and follow Jesus. He will prove to you He is God and give you eternal life.

The Bible says God desires all men to be saved and to come to the full knowledge of the truth (1 Timothy 2:4).

God wants you to know who He is! He wants to demonstrate his power to you. Maybe you have tried and failed to find God through religion or philosophy. God wants to show You that He is alive. He does miracles. He wants to prove to you that He is everything you are looking for.

I remember when I had just commenced Seminary at Oral Roberts University, I went away to pray and spend time at the International House of Prayer in Kansas City. This is a place where they have, 24 hours 7 days a week, worship and intercession. There is an incredible presence of God in that place. I prayed there for two days and nights and the third night I had an encounter with God, which changed my life forever.

As I was praying, a young pastor prayed for me, and I felt the power of God begin to shake me. I fell on the ground like a dead man and began shaking and crying out wondering what was happening. I looked up and I saw a vision of Jesus. He was looking at me and His eyes were a flame of fire. I could see He was standing in the midst of a fire.

As I looked into His eyes I felt the fire burning in my eyes and my mind and the fire was burning me up. I looked for as long as I could into those eyes until I had to look down, I couldn't take it any more. I couldn't take anymore of that fire.

Every time I looked down, my eyes were drawn back to those eyes of fire like a magnet. I would look into those eyes for as long as I could until I had to look away again. This encounter continued for one hour, this looking into the eyes of fire. Two hours passed and still the eyes continued to burn in me. Three hours passed and I was beginning to wonder when this encounter would stop.

After four hours I began saying God I can't take anymore. I said, "what are you doing to me?" I felt God speak to me and say, "I'm setting you on fire again." God was burning me up, preparing me for ministry. I had spent all those years in the corporate world in New Zealand and London and I was feeling all of the things I had been doing being burned up with the fire of God. I had lost my first love. I had lost my zeal for God and the things of God. God was doing something to change me. I believe this is what happened to Peter and the disciples on the birthday of the Church, Pentecost.

Before the fire of God fell at Pentecost, the disciples of Jesus were hidden away in their houses unsure of what to do. Peter had denied Christ. They were living in fear and timidity. They weren't sure what they believed and there was no way they were going to convince anyone of God's reality or of the truths of the claims of Christianity.

All of a sudden, when that Pentecostal fire fell on their lives, they became bold witnesses to the resurrection, many people responded when they saw the miracles and heard that bold, powerful and anointed preaching. The fire began to touch their lives as they saw and heard what God was doing. They were convinced as the fire of God fell from heaven on their lives as well.

When I began to ponder what had happened to me in my encounter with Jesus, the man of fire, I began to search the Scriptures. Throughout scriptures, some of the prophets had heavenly visitations and visions and saw similar visions of Jesus and had had encounter with the God who is a consuming fire.

The Prophet Ezekiel had the following vision of Jesus:

In the sixth year, in the sixth month, on the fifth day, while I was sitting in my house, and the elders of Judah were sitting before me, the hand of the Sovereign LORD came upon me there.

I looked, and saw a figure like that of a man. From what appeared to be his waist down he was like fire, and from there up his appearance was as bright as glowing metal.
                                                    Ezekiel 8:1,2

The Prophet Daniel had similar visions of Jesus:

"As I looked the thrones were set in place, and the Ancient of days took his seat. His clothing was white as snow; and the hair of his head was like white wool:

His throne was flaming with fire, and it's wheels were all ablaze."
                                                          Daniel 7:9

I looked up and there before me was a man dressed in linen, with a belt of the finest gold around his waist.

His body was like chrysolite, and his face like lightning, his eyes like flaming torches, his arms and legs like the gleam of burnished bronze, and his voice like the voice of a multitude.

I Daniel was the only one who saw the vision: the men with me did not see it but such terror overwhelmed them that they fled and hid themselves.
                                                       Daniel 10:5-7

The Apostle John had an incredible vision of Jesus while he was in exile on the island of Patmos which shook him to the core:

I turned to see the voice that was speaking to me. And when I turned, I saw seven golden lampstands;

and amongst the lampstands was someone like a son of man, dressed in a robe reaching down to his foot, and with a golden sash around his chest.

His head and hair were white like wool, as white as snow; and his eyes were like a blazing fire.

His feet were bronze, glowing in a furnace; and his voice was like the sound of rushing waters.

In his right hand he held the seven stars: and out of his mouth came a sharp double-edged sword. His face was like the sun shining in all it's brilliance.

When I saw him, I fell at his feet as though dead. Then he placed his right hand on me, and said: "Do not be afraid. I am the First and the Last.

I am the Living One; I was dead, and behold, I am alive for ever and ever!"
                                              Revelation 1:12-18

Jesus is incredible to behold. These Prophets and Apostles had encounters and saw visions of Jesus which radically transformed their lives. They were totally overwhelmed. Jesus appeared to these people to reveal His awesomeness, His majesty, and His holiness. All of the visions are similar and Jesus is still the same today He wants to reveal Himself to you, to radically transform your life and set you ablaze.

Jesus was looking at John and looking at the early Church with eyes of fire. These eyes cannot look upon sin, and the fire in His eyes purges away every form of evil and dross. Jesus had messages for the Church. He wanted them to repent of their lukewarm hearts or their materialism or whatever other area of their hearts had been infiltrated by sin and compromise.

I'm not sure I can explain too well exactly what happened to me during the encounter I had with those eyes of fire. I can only say it transformed my life forever. Every time I have been up to preach there is a dynamic power that is released. God's fire, conviction of sin and a transforming power is released into the lives of those we have been ministering to.

We have traveled to the nations of the world preaching the Gospel and seen people who have never met God before have encounters with His reality and His fire. People have been coming up to the stage and asking "what is happening to me? I have never experienced anything like this before. What is this fire burning in my heart?" I'm telling you God is real! His power can be experienced by anyone and everyone.

When you have a supernatural encounter with the God who answers by fire, you will never be the same again. God will change you, he will revolutionize you. The fire of God is a fierce and passionate love from God.

It is His fierce and passionate love for you! In the Bible in the Song of Solomon 8:6 we read:

Place me like a seal over your heart, like a seal over your arm; for love is as strong as death, its jealousy as unyielding as the grave, it burns like a blazing fire, like a mighty flame.

God wants us to experience a fire in our hearts, which represents His fierce love for us, and in turn a fierce love for Him. How much does God love you and how much do you love God? You need the fire of God to begin to burn in your heart and reveal the love of God to you.

Let Jesus look at you with His eyes of fire as you read this book and place a fresh love in your heart for Him. Maybe you don't believe in God. We have seen many people who have no faith in God have this kind of experience in their hearts as the fire of God has ignited their hearts. The first commandment God gave to humanity was to love God with all your heart. This is what God looks for more than anything else, and He wants you to experience His fiery love.

The fire of God is a hunger for the things of God. Jesus said:

Blessed are they that hunger and thirst for right-eousness for they will be filled.
                                                    Matthew 5:6

Maybe you have no desire for God or no interest in God. As the fire of God touches your life, all that will change in an instant; there will be a hunger for the things of God.

The fire of God is the purifying, sanctifying work of the Holy Spirit, a refining fire. Malachi 3:2 states:

> **But who can endure the day of his coming? Who can
> stand when he appears? For he will be like a refiner's
> fire or a launderer's soap.**

God, by His very nature, is holy, He works with people who, by their nature, are impure, so He comes like a
launderer's soap and a purifying fire to clean out our lives
and burn up the impurities. Remember it is God who
does this work of purifying, all we need to do is allow
Him to have His way.

John the Baptist spoke about Jesus in Matthew 3:11,12
saying:

> **"I baptize you with water for repentance. But after
> me will come one who is more powerful than I whose
> sandals I am not fit to carry. He will baptize you with
> the Holy Spirit and with fire.**

> **His winnowing fork is in His hand, and He will
> clear His threshing floor, gathering his wheat into his
> barn and burning up the chaff with unquenchable fire."**

Jesus' job is to purify and cleanse us. He won't allow
any sin in our lives. We need to lay our lives bare before
Him and let him burn up all the chaff and all the impu-
rity in our lives so we can walk before Him in holiness.
God wants you to be holy just like He is holy. I'm believ-
ing this fire will begin to burn in your heart as Jesus
Himself draws near to you as you read this book and that
God will show you He is real.

Maybe you are convinced that God is real, however
you are not convinced Christianity is the way to connect
with God. I am trusting that God will answer in your life
by fire like He has in my life and in the lives of countless
others to prove to you that Christianity is the way to go.
I believe God will convince you of the truths of the
claims of Christianity.

Chapter 8
Revival and the Reality of God

I believe we live in a Thomas generation, a generation of people who need to see something substantial before they can really believe. People are looking for an encounter, an encounter which convinces them that God is real.

Revival is a time where God begins to manifest Himself supernaturally and if you are not a Christian and you are reading this book, I am believing God's manifest presence will be felt by you at this time. When God begins to move in revival not just individuals are affected, but entire nations are affected. Everyone is affected by a great movement of the Spirit of God.

Throughout history, there have been many times where God seems to draw near to cities and different nations and pour out His Spirit in greater measure. This phenomenon is known as revival. Many of the revivals of previous decades have changed entire nations.

The Welsh revival had a tremendous impact on the country of Wales. It is estimated that between the years of 1904-1905 as many as 152,000 people in Wales came to a saving knowledge of Jesus Christ. There were approximately 1.7 million people who lived in Wales at the time, so the percentage impacted was in the region of eight percent of the total population.

God used the young preacher Evan Roberts to spread the effects of this revival. Four years prior to the commencement of the Welsh revival. "Seth Joshua, a leading Bible teacher, had prayed, asking God to select some able person to present revival truths. The Lord answered him by calling Evan Roberts."[27]

Evan Roberts himself had been praying for years for revival. In the spring of 1904, Roberts had a series of life changing encounters with the Holy Spirit of God. Penn-Lewis a friend of Roberts describes the encounters as follows:

"God seems to have drawn near to him in a very special way. He says that as he prayed by his bedside at night, he was taken up into a great expanse, without space or time, into communion with God.... After this the Lord awakened him night after night a little after one o'clock, and took him up into Divine fellowship for about four hours. He would sleep until nine o'clock, when he would be rapt in communion with God until about noon on the day."[28]

Evan Roberts went to a preparatory school for ministry in the town of Newcastle Emlyn in Wales. Roberts never completed his studies at the preparatory school, however it was at the school that the Holy Spirit began to speak to him to go back to his own people and preach to them the things that God had laid on his heart. When Roberts eventually yielded to the prompting of the Holy Spirit in the chapel where he was praying, "the glory of the Lord so filled the chapel that he could not see for the glory of that light."[29]

In obedience to God, Roberts went to his hometown in Loughor, where he called a meeting in his church for all the young people. An account of one of these early meetings is as follows:

"Slowly and quietly — for it must be emphasized that fluency of speech had never been a marked characteristic of his — he spoke of the deep things of God and Christ, the hours passing quite unobserved, while tears coursed uninterruptedly over the cheeks of his listeners. People passing by the church commented freely and wonderingly upon the unusual spectacle of lights burning in full blaze at such an hour.... Inside the building strange things were happening. Young men and women who had never been known to speak openly of any experience of saving grace stood and testified fearlessly. Others were bowed in prayer. Some sang the hymns of Zion. Tears, sobs, and songs of praise were intermingled, continuing until near midnight. The happy throng dispersed in all directions.... Next day the village was agog. When Mr. Roberts arrived for the pre-arranged service next evening, the chapel was besieged with curious worshippers, hardly knowing what would transpire.... When it became known that some of the outstanding characters of the neighborhood had been converted after withstanding Gospel appeals of eminent preachers for a lifetime, and that these were declaring new-found joy and faith without shame or fear, the excitement became tense. Rumors sped far and wide. Down in the bowels of the Earth, miners not only discussed the services but actually sang boisterously the grand old hymns taught them in their childhood."[30]

A personal account from Roberts concerning one of the early meetings was, "after many had prayed, I felt some living energy or force entering my bosom, restraining my breath, my legs trembled terribly; this living energy increased as one after another prayed. Feeling strongly and deeply warmed, I burst forth in prayer."[31]

The main topic of Roberts' preaching and teaching was revival and obedience to the Holy Spirit. One of the famous prayers of Evan Roberts' was "Bend the Church." The prayer "Bend the Church" being a prayer that God would bring His Church in submission to the will of the Holy Spirit. Roberts would lead the meetings praying "Plyg ni, O Arglwydd!" — "Bend us, O Lord." Roberts' placing of the Holy Spirit as pre-eminent in his meetings gave the freedom for the Holy Spirit to move in power, shaking literally thousands of believers and unbelievers alike.

The early believers obeyed the Holy Spirit and were heavily reliant on the Holy Spirit. It is almost as if when believers are prepared to put God first and give the Holy Spirit his rightful place in the Church, He will move in mighty power.

During the revival, the chapel, from which Roberts preached, was kept open day and night, so that worshippers could go there to pray and praise God. The changes in the life of the town were dramatic. "Everything sprang into new life. Former blasphemers were the most eloquent, both in prayer and praise.... Drunkards forgot the way to saloons...they were busy worshipping.... It was the young people who responded with the greatest alacrity to the challenge of absolute surrender and consecrated to the service of the Lord.... With ever increasing momentum, the movement advanced, creating unprecedented excitement among the churches and the secular institutions outside."[32]

The bars were emptied, dance halls, theatres and football matches all saw dramatic decline in attendance. Long-standing debts were repaid, church and family feuds were healed and a new unity of purpose was felt across denominational divides.[33]

The revival spread to many parts of Wales not just the counties where Roberts was preaching. "The fire of God burned in towns and villages which he did not visit. Many of the places he did visit, he found the fire was already there. His visit only fanned the flame."[34]

Stewart researched the revival and found from looking at newspapers at the time of the revival, that there were no advertisements advertising the revival. He was struck by the "lack of commercialism." According to Stewart there were "no hymn books, no song leaders, no committees, no choirs, no great preachers, no offerings and no organization."[35]

The Holy Spirit orchestrated the revival. It seemed that Roberts had an aversion to planned events and would prefer to allow the Holy Spirit to direct proceedings. Roberts was a quiet humble man and some writers argue that this was the reason that God chose him to be a key figure in the revival. The Scripture says that, "God chooses the weak things of this world to shame the strong" (1 Corinthians 1:27). There are reports that at times he would not preach but would stand at the pulpit and just weep. As he wept, the power of God fell. God does not need our many words necessarily, He just needs a humble broken heart, someone that is sold out to Him and is willing to be a fool for Christ.

The Apostle Paul said that he came not with "wise and persuasive words, but with the demonstration of Spirit's power" (1 Corinthians 2:4). The Apostle Paul knew in his day that more than words were needed to convince people of the existence of God.

As we consider what God has done in history, we need to understand and know that He can do it again. I believe He can and that He will, I believe we are in a season of revival and end-time harvest. The greatest outpouring of God's Spirit in human history is about to take place. God has heard the cry of His people, the wickedness on the earth is increasing.

Like it was in the days of Noah, so it will be in the days of the Son of man. In the days of Noah, the wickedness on the earth had increased to the point that God made the decision to destroy the earth with a great flood. Only Noah and his family were spared. For forty days and nights the earth and the heavens opened and the earth was covered with water.

It is my belief that God will not judge the earth with a flood of water again, but will come to fix the problems of humanity this time with a great flood of His Spirit. Every inch of the earth will be covered with the Spirit of God. No one will stand in God's way; no kingdom, king, queen, principality or power.

I believe God's Spirit will go into the highways and the byways; into the streets, the bars and the restaurants. It will go into the darkest and most impossible places, where people's lives are ruins and ashes, God will make something beautiful out of their lives.

In the days of Noah, no one had ever seen a flood of that magnitude before. This outpouring will be similar. It will be the greatest outpouring ever to flood the Earth. It will break out from the depths of the Church; pouring like rain and breaking from depths of the lives of believers and flooding the Earth.

Noah had a word from God that God would flood the Earth. In the same way God is speaking to many that He will flood the Earth with revival. People may say, "where is it?" When God speaks like He did to Noah, we need to continue to believe it will happen.

In Noah's time the waters broke forth from the deep and the rain came down. In similar manner I believe, the foundations of the deep break forth. The earth shall be covered with the floods of God. People will want to run to the Ark of salvation to be saved. All that God says is evil shall be purged and swallowed up with the floods of God. Cities and entire nations will be covered with the floods of God's Spirit.

When God does something big, we need to be prepared to wait and obey; hold fast to what God has spoken, not letting the discouragement of those who do not believe to affect us. When the floods come, they will be forced to believe.

"You heavens above, rain down righteousness; let the clouds shower it down. Let the earth open wide, let salvation spring up, let righteousness grow up with it, I the Lord, have created it."
                                                    Isaiah 45:8

Ask the Lord for rain in the springtime; it is the Lord who makes the storm clouds; He gives showers of rain to men, and plants of the field to everyone.
                                                    Zechariah 10:1

In the revivals of past history, there are things which happened which no one could stop, which were unstoppable. Maybe you don't know God, but I want to tell you something happens when God's people begin to pray.

Revival is also ignited when God's people suffer persecution and various trials. In my personal life I have had to walk through some tough times, some refining processes. I can testify that as I walked through these times I have met Jesus. There is a story in the Bible of three Hebrew children who dared to defy the king of the day and were thrown into a fiery furnace and had the trial of their lives.

It was in the fire that they met Jesus. As we dare to obey God and not man and walk through the fiery trials of life, we meet with Jesus in the midst of the fire. As I and those connected with me in ministry have dared to walk into the fire, the fire of God has exploded wherever we go.

We have been to India, Central and South America, as well as all over the United States of America. Let me share some stories with you of what God has been doing. In India we had an Evangelistic Campaign where everyone, believers and non-believers alike encountered the fire of God.

On the third night we felt very impressed that God was speaking about revival and the fire of God for the city. I preached on the fire of God and asked all the pastors of the city to come forward for prayer. We saw the fire of God fall on the pastors. Many of the pastors began to weep as the fire of God fell on them. Others fell down under the weight of God's glory. There was a great work of God's Spirit to bring unity between the pastors of the city.

We had a testimony from a woman in the crowd who saw fire from heaven fall on her, and as it hit her she fell rolling around on the ground. She testified that she came to the meeting with many things she needed from God and with a great hunger for Him. She said her experience with God's fire answered all of her prayers and desires in an instant!

Recently we were in Bolivia and we had another campaign there. I preached in a church on the Thursday night prior to the campaign and a pastor from another church brought some youth with him, some saved and some unsaved. He later shared that the fire of the Holy

Spirit had fallen on the unsaved youth and that they were so impacted they later gave their hearts to Christ.

At the crusade, we had people who had never encountered God before in their lives come up and share how the fire of the Holy Spirit had fallen on them during the meeting, and they encountered the reality of God for the first time. They wept as they made their decisions for Christ. We had one man who came to the meeting with bitterness and unforgiveness in his heart. He shared that he wept the entire time the message was being preached. He felt the fire of God burning up inside his heart, burning up all the unforgiveness and bitterness, transforming his life.

On the first night of the campaign we had a little boy come up and share how his sight had been healed. He had been partially blind, had glasses about a fourth inch thick and didn't need them anymore. His eyes shone as he looked around, being able to see properly for the first time. We had other people come up and testify of being healed of partial blindness, deafness and paralysis. People testified of the fire of God falling on them and healing them. There were so many miracle testimonies, we didn't have time for everyone to come on to the stage to testify. When God's Spirit begins to move, unprecedented miracles begin to happen.

On the final night of the campaign we saw many more healing miracles. One lady who was paralyzed had been prayed for the previous night and she was able to walk a few steps while we held her up. I told her to come back on the final night. We prayed for her again and she was able to walk unassisted across the length of the campaign grounds!

Six weeks later, people were still being impacted by the fire of God. There was a young lady who lived on the other side of Bolivia, and at the time of our evangelistic campaign she was visiting the area in El Alto, Bolivia. She helped us translate during the campaign, and believe it or not, she was not very open to God's power and was resisting it in her heart. After some exposure to the presence, power and fire of God, the fire began to consume her life and now she is sharing it with others.

She wrote to the ministry, "I will never stop glorifying God for what He did with me through you. My love for Him is growing more and more because of what He is doing with me. Everyday, He has something new for me. On Sunday I preached in my church and seven young people and also my pastor received the Holy Spirit and God's fire. He takes me different places and introduces me to people to talk them about Him and His love."

In the United States, as we have traveled and ministered in the various churches, we have seen similar things happen. What happens continues to have a reverberating effect. It is the beginning of something huge. In Michigan we have had many opportunities to minister, one of the more memorable times was at the Assemblies of God — Alma Mount Hope Church. May Vankempen is a member of that church and she shared the following with me a few days later:

"While you were ministering, in a vision I saw a big ball of fire, bigger than the room, come down and started coming from the front to the back covering the whole building. The fire was consuming everyone's bad spirits and started making people get their joy back. It seemed to me the church was about ready to die. When you came to our church that's when it hit. I got hit hard by the fire of God for the first time in my life. On Sunday everybody was still experiencing the power of God —

God continued to visit. Even the youth were experiencing the tangible presence of God — they weren't there on Wednesday night. I believe the youth and everyone will grow now. It seemed to me we were just dead, in my own life I felt like I was dead spiritually, kind of lost. I feel like God has given me a new spiritual heart."

Wherever we have gone we have seen people shaken with the power and fire of God. It has been a humbling experience to watch God move so powerfully. I believe God wants to do something in the world today. He is looking for people who are willing to be radically obedient to Him and the leading of His Spirit, to be willing to follow Him wherever He leads, to do whatever He says.

Sometimes when you follow God, things just begin to get worse, they begin to get more difficult. Just when you thought things couldn't get any worse, they do! There are times when God will test your obedience to Him. He may lead you to a place of adversity, to the point you are staring death in the face. Will you obey God or will you obey man, yourself or the devil?

Earlier in this book we considered the story of Job. God said Job was someone who walked perfectly before God and as he did he began to go through the most horrendous trial. He lost his children, his business, everything! God led him through an incredible test, which ultimately resulted in him drawing closer to God. He had an encounter with God which shook him to the core. God appeared to Him in a whirlwind. Sometimes God will lead us through a fiery trial before we have an incredible encounter with Him.

Before Jesus entered into His public ministry, a ministry which was marked by the supernatural power of God, God led Him into a time of testing. He was led into the wilderness, and at the end of His fasting when

He was at His weakest, the devil came to Him and tested Him, and tried Him. It was not until He was led through a period of intense testing that God released Him into public ministry.

Jesus was led to the Cross and was willing to die in order to stay in the will of God. He prayed "not My will but Your will be done." The Apostle Peter tried to dissuade Jesus from going to the cross, but Peter didn't understand that sometimes suffering can be part of the will of God. Jesus died on that cross and yet even death did not stop a miracle from happening. It took courage to do that. To die and face death and torture. Even in death and torture He was in the will of God! What He did released such power it changed the course of human history.

Consider with me the story of the three Hebrew children in Daniel 3. The Hebrew children refused to obey the decree of the king to bow down and worship the golden idol which he had made, and because they refused, he threatened to throw them into a fiery furnace. They replied:

..."O Nebuchanezzar, we do not need to defend ourselves before you in this matter.

If we are thrown into the blazing furnace, the God we serve is able to save us from it, and he will rescue us from your hand, O king.

But if he does we want you to know O king that we will not serve your gods, or worship the image of gold you have set up."
                                        Daniel 3:16-18

After these three Hebrew children were thrown into the fire and the King looked into the fire and said:

...**"Look! I see four men walking around in the fire, unbound and unharmed, and the fourth looks like a son of the gods."**

Daniel 3:25

God showed up and delivered them and they came out of that fire completely free, unharmed and without even the smell of smoke on their clothes.

There are many times we are put into a situation where there is no hope, we are facing a fire. We have to be willing to follow God wherever He leads. This was real fire, we are talking about the spiritual fire of God, but there are some things in this passage which will help us encounter and walk in the fire of God.

It takes courage to stand and face possible death and know that unless God does a miracle I'm dead. This was real fire and, unless God intervened, they would have been dead within moments. If you bow to this fear you will burn, if you don't bow God will move heaven and earth to show up with a miracle, and walk with you like the fourth man. You need to be willing to obey God. If you don't bow Jesus will step in.

As the children were thrown into the fire, they were bound and held by guards. The guards were killed as they threw them into the fire and they went into the fire bound but came out loosed. The fire of God will break every chain in your life. Every bondage of sin, every sickness, every disease and poverty, whatever is binding you will be burned up with fire; God wants to set you free.

We should never be moved by circumstances, but only by the Word of God. The fire is not always something we enjoy; it burns up the flesh and sin in our life. Are you willing to walk into the fire? This was a supernatural miracle, yes they were delivered from the fire, but they had to be willing to walk into the fire. If you are willing to walk into the fire your miracle will happen. Jesus was waiting for them in the fire. He is waiting there for you.

All of these people were willing to go through the refining fires, the refining processes of God in order to release what God was wanting to do. They were willing to go to the point of death. To die to their own will and desires and do the will of God. This is the kind of faith God is looking for. He wants to bring His people close to Him to that place of fire and allow Him to do a miracle in their lives.

Throughout the centuries we see that Christianity has exploded under persecution. As God's people have come under fire, and walked through the fire, the fire of Christianity has spread. As believers have been killed and died for their faith, their deaths have resulted in a tremendous explosion of Christianity. No child of God ever suffers, or no one who dies for the Gospel, does that in vain. As God's people are willing to follow God wherever He leads, God begins to release His power and glory.

In China the church has suffered intense persecution and in the midst of the suffering there has been explosion of growth. The story of the Christian Church in China oppressed under Communism is inspiring. Communist regimes such as those in China always regard Christianity as a threat to their very existence, because of their atheistic political ideology.

During the dark years of Mao's *Great Leap Forward* (launched in 1958) and *The Great Proletarian Cultural Revolution* (1966), multitudes of Christian leaders were killed and imprisoned for their faith, and many others spent years in hard labor camps. The communists thought they were destroying the Church, but all their repressive actions did was release more of God's presence and power.

The Church in China sprang quietly to life like a freshly sown field. Led primarily by elderly women who had escaped the communist purges, small house churches sprouted all over the country. Their very existence was and still is illegal. Fifty years of oppression and persecution have seen this Church grow from around one million believers in 1949 to approximately 100 million today. The Communists and others have tried to stop God, however, no matter how hard you try, God is unstoppable.

Chapter 9
Jesus and the Reality of God

Jesus died and rose from the dead, a total miracle of God. He is still active in this world today performing miracles and demonstrating His reality. In the previous chapter we discussed the fire of God. When Jesus rose from the dead, He left a deposit of the fire of God in the hearts of His disciples.

In the book of Luke 24:13-34 we read:

Now that same day two of them were going to a village called Emmaus, about seven miles from Jerusalem.

They were talking with each other about everything that had happened.

As they talked and discussed these things with each other, Jesus himself came up and walked along with them;

but they were kept from recognizing him.

He asked them, "What are you discussing together as you walk along?" They stood still, their faces downcast.

One of them, named Cleopas, asked him, "Are you only a visitor to Jerusalem and do not know the things that have happened there in these days?"

"What things?" he asked. "About Jesus of Nazareth," they replied. "He was a prophet, powerful in word and deed before God and all the people.

The chief priests and our rulers handed him over to be sentenced to death, and they crucified him;

but we had hoped that he was the one who was going to redeem Israel. And what is more, it is the third day since all this took place.

In addition, some of our women amazed us. They went to the tomb early this morning

but didn't find his body. They came and told us that they had seen a vision of angels, who said he was alive.

Then some of our companions went to the tomb and found it just as the women had said, but him they did not see."

He said to them, "How foolish you are, and how slow of heart to believe all that the prophets have spoken!

Did not the Christ have to suffer these things and then enter his glory?"

And beginning with Moses and all the Prophets, he explained to them what was said in all the Scriptures concerning himself.

As they approached the village to which they were going, Jesus acted as if he were going farther.

But they urged him strongly, "Stay with us, for it is nearly evening; the day is almost over." So he went in to stay with them.

When he was at the table with them, he took bread, gave thanks, broke it and began to give it to them.

Then their eyes were opened and they recognized him, and he disappeared from their sight.

They asked each other, "Were not our hearts burning within us while he talked with us on the road and opened the Scriptures to us?"

They got up and returned at once to Jerusalem. There they found the Eleven and those with them, assembled together

and saying, "It is true! The Lord has risen and has appeared to Simon."

These disciples of Jesus thought He was dead. They had some understanding of who Jesus was and what His mission was, but they lacked a complete understanding. They had been expecting a leader who would redeem Israel; more of a political figure. As they pondered His death and what had happened, Jesus Himself showed up.

However their eyes were kept from seeing him. Maybe that's you, maybe you have serious questions about Jesus Christ. Maybe you are pondering in your heart, who is this Jesus Christ. I am believing that as you do, Jesus Himself will draw near to you and begin to answer your questions. I believe God wants us to discover things for ourselves. Maybe your eyes have been kept from seeing Jesus Christ, but I am trusting He will reveal Himself to you. It is as we begin to ponder the issues of life, of who He is, that he begins to work and lead us into all truth.

Jesus began to explain to them how He needed to suffer and die and rise from the dead. They were looking for a political revolution, but as we will see, Jesus came to bring a revolution of the heart. There are many prophecies, some of them thousands of years old, which were fulfilled in the coming of Christ. Jesus shared these things to His disciples. Some of the things He may have shared are:

• At the ancient Jewish feast of Passover, a lamb in perfect condition had to be killed (Exodus 12:3-6); this was fulfilled and represented by the sacrifice of Jesus, "the Lamb of God, who takes away the sin of the world" (John 1:29; 1 Corinthians 5:7). The spotless condition which was required for all the animal sacrifices pointed forward to the perfect character of Jesus (Exodus 12:5; 1 Peter 1:19). Jesus was the ultimate sacrifice for the sin of humanity.

• Throughout the Psalms and prophets of the Old Testament there are countless prophecies about what Jesus would be like. They particularly focus on describing how He would die.

• In Psalms 22:1 it says, "My God, my God, why have you forsaken me?" The fulfillment of this is that these were the exact words of Jesus used when He died on the cross (Matthew 27:46).

• In Psalm 22:6-8 it says, "But I am a worm and not a man, scorned by men and despised by the people. All who see me mock me; they hurl insults, shaking their heads: 'He trusts in the LORD; let the LORD rescue him. Let him deliver him, since he delights in him.'" The fulfillment of this is that Jesus' own people despised and mocked Him (Luke 23:35; 8:53); they shook their heads (Matthew 27:39), and said these words as Jesus hung on the cross (Matthew 27:43).

• In Psalm 22:15,16 it says, "My tongue sticks to the roof of my mouth…they have pierced my hands and my feet." This was fulfilled in Christ's thirst on the cross (John 19:28). The piercing of hands and feet refers to the physical method of crucifixion used.

• In Psalm 22:18 it says, "They divide my garments among them and cast lots for my clothing." The precise

86

fulfillment of this is found in Matthew 27:35, the description of what the soldiers did at the foot of the cross with the garments of Jesus.

• In Psalm 69:21 it says, "They put gall in my food and gave me vinegar for my thirst." This was fulfilled when Christ was on the cross (Matthew 27:34).

The whole of Isaiah 53 is an incredible prophecy describing in vivid detail Christ's death and resurrection. Nearly every verse mentioned has had an unmistakable fulfillment in the coming of Christ.

• In Isaiah 53:7 it says, "As a sheep before her shearers is silent, so he did not open his mouth." This was fulfilled by Christ, the Lamb of God, who remained silent during the entire proceedings of His trial. He was like a lamb led to the slaughter, they spat on Him, accused Him falsely and the entire time He did not respond (Matthew 27:12,14).

• In Isaiah 53:9 it says, "He was assigned a grave with the wicked, and with the rich in his death." This was fulfilled when Jesus was crucified alongside criminals, who freely admitted they deserved their own fate, while Jesus did not (Matthew 27:38). In addition Jesus was buried in the tomb of a rich man (Matthew 27:57-60).

As Jesus began to share these things with the disciples from Scripture, they later said to each other "did not our hearts burn within us, while he talked with us and opened the scriptures to us?" There was something stirring in their hearts as the truth of Christ was presented to them by Christ Himself. I am trusting God that He will do the same for you. As you ponder who Christ is, my prayer is that you will feel a stirring and a burning in your heart for God and the truth.

Jesus was the manifestation, the fulfillment of God's promises to humanity. He was God's Word coming into the world in human form. God had a plan from ages past to send Christ, the promised one, the anointed one, the Messiah to redeem humanity because He saw all of the problems we faced.

Our world seems stricken with pain, disease, trauma and war. The problems of this world seem insurmountable. God never intended for things to be this way. The disease of sin has infiltrated the human race. God wants to step down to this earth from heaven and transform everything with a miracle to bringing healing and hope. This is what Jesus Christ did.

Jesus was born into this world with a mission to redeem fallen humanity. He came to die for us, and as He died on the cross, He took upon Himself all the sin and affects of the fall as an atonement for sin. By faith we can appropriate the benefits of this saving act. Jesus died to bring new and eternal life instead of spiritual and eternal death (John 3:16), healing instead of sickness (Matthew 8:17), prosperity instead of poverty (2 Corinthians 8:9), and restoration to relationship with God.

As Jesus died, the veil of the temple was torn asunder (Matthew 27:51) meaning that God would no longer dwell in tabernacles made of human hands, but that He would make His children the temple of the Holy Spirit (1 Corinthians 3:16). The rending of the veil also means we have the ability to come into the holy presence of God and experience once again intimacy and relationship with God, to bask in the glory of God and experience communion and intimacy with God just as Adam and Eve did before the fall.

The purpose of Jesus Christ was to bring salvation to hurting humanity. Jesus' mission was to bring life and health in this present life and in eternity. God wants you to spend eternity in heaven with Him when this life is over.

God wants to change this world to show suffering people that He doesn't want things to be that way. He weeps over our pain and our suffering, He knows what suffering is. He suffered for all of us. I remember when I lived in London, sitting in the living room of my apartment talking to my roommate. He was a young man contemplating life and he said, "please explain to me where God is in the midst of all the suffering in this world? I just don't understand it."

I said to him, "if you listen quietly enough, really quietly, you will hear the sound of the cries of Christ as they nail Him to the cross." The "noise" and busyness of this world drown out those cries of anguish, so that this young man could not hear. People refuse to believe that God cares, but this is where He is in the midst of suffering. He identified with the suffering of humanity at the cross.

When we see the suffering of humanity, we know God cares. He may not respond when and how we would like Him to, but He cares and knows. Jesus went to the Cross to identify with our pain. Many people don't see or understand what Christ has done, we live in an age which denies the very existence and reality of God.

When Jesus came to the earth many people doubted Jesus was the Son of the Living God. At one point, the Jews were ready to stone Him because of this claim, but Jesus did so many supernatural things to convince others that He was the Messiah. There are many passages of Scripture which attest to this.

"Believe me when I say that I am in the Father and the Father is in me or believe on the evidence of the miracles themselves."
John 14:11

…"I am the way and the truth and the life. No one comes to the Father except through me."

John 14:6

Now while he was in Jerusalem at the Passover Feast, many people saw the miraculous signs he was doing and believed in his name.

John 2:23

He came to Jesus at night and said, "Rabbi, we know you are a teacher who has come from God. For no one could perform the miraculous signs you are doing if God were not with him.

John 3:2

and a great crowd of people followed him because they saw the miraculous signs he had performed on the sick.

John 6:2

Still, many in the crowd put their faith in him. They said, "When the Christ comes, will he do more miraculous signs than this man?"

John 7:31

"Men of Israel, listen to this: Jesus of Nazareth was a man accredited by God to you by miracles, wonders and signs, which God did among you through him, as you yourselves know."

Acts 2:22

Jesus Christ is the same yesterday, today, and forever.

Hebrews 13:8

This basically means that Jesus still does today what He did in Bible days. There are many Christians in this world today who believe that miracles are for today. The fastest growing segment of Christianity is comprised of those who believe Jesus still does miracles.

Although society has become more complex and closed to the message of Christianity, the same basic needs for a supernatural encounter with God remains.

People have a need and Jesus is willing to meet that need. Jesus is more than a good teacher, or philosopher. He is the risen Son of God and He will use miracles today to prove that He exists.

You can call out upon the name of many gods in your life, and believe in many different philosophies, but it is only when you call out the Name of Jesus there will be an answer. Jesus answers like no other god. Answers to prayer come from a relationship with Jesus Christ.

Jesus was God incarnate. His birth was a miracle, His life and ministry demonstrated miracles and His resurrection was a miracle. The Creation event was a miracle. God is a supernatural God who does miracles. Miracles are used by God to demonstrate His reality. God is more real than we are. Miracles are when God touches the ugliness of this unreal world and transforms it into something beautiful. They are acts of the love and compassion of God. They are acts of a God who is merciful, a God who understands the pain and suffering of humanity.

All this life is just a shadow of God and His Kingdom. God does not need to be defended. He will prove Himself real. What does that mean? We have no idea who God is. We often misrepresent Him to others. The miracles of Jesus prove to us He is the only way to the Father. People followed and believed in Jesus Christ because of the miracles He did. His power has not changed to heal the sick and diseased.

Jesus Christ, the Son of God, is a miracle worker and He wants to prove to you that He is real, that He is alive. His miracles prove to those who don't know Him that He is the only way to God. If you are struggling with sickness and you are reading this book, Jesus can do a miracle for you. If you are struggling with a crippling

91

disease, Jesus can do a miracle for you. If you have given up hope that you will ever see or hear, Jesus can do a miracle for you.

God is a God of compassion. He is all powerful and His Kingdom brings freedom to all those who are bound by the power of the enemy. God wants you to be free from all forms of oppression. He wants to heal your physical body and save your eternal soul.

I want to challenge you. Are you willing to believe the claims of Christ? Are you willing to believe He will meet you where you are and give you the miracle you need? Where is your heart as you read this book? God is calling you to Himself. I want to challenge you to take this message seriously. God wants to meet you right where you are.

I recall the story of a man we had at one our meetings, in Auckland, New Zealand. He was an Indian man, a Hindu. He came in a wheelchair. His wife was pushing the chair. He had just had three heart attacks and two strokes. He was cross-eyed and unable to talk. We felt the compassion of God for this man. Jesus wanted to heal him. We prayed and asked God to restore his health.

We later found out that Jesus Christ had appeared to him in a vision and told him to come to our meeting for prayer. This man went home the same way he came to the meeting, the miracle was not instantaneous. However, he came to our next meeting completely restored, his eyes were perfect, he could walk and he could speak. This is what Jesus Christ wants to do for you. He wants to make you whole. Put your trust and faith in Jesus Christ for the miracle you need.

Miracles are used to demonstrate the reality of God, that He is more real than we are. His world is more real than our world, it is heaven. Heaven is a place where there is no sorrow, no suffering, no pain or disease. Jesus saw the suffering of this world and wanted to bring us relief from it. He died in our place suffering on the cross for our sins, so that we could be reinstated as citizens of heaven.

I spent one and one half years preaching the Gospel on the streets of New Zealand and have worked with a number of different evangelists. I found that the people of New Zealand are very tough minded, and many are resistant to the concept of God and Christianity. I can tell you from my experience that even in spite of this resistance, there is a hunger and a desire in the human heart for the supernatural, for an encounter with God. Many people need to see something before they can believe, they need to see a demonstration of the supernatural.

Many people want to believe God exists but their philosophical framework restricts them. Like Thomas, they need to see before they can believe. I believe Jesus hears this cry of the human heart and is willing to meet people right where they are. He is willing to meet you right where you are.

Chapter 10
The Holy Spirit and the Reality of God

The Holy Spirit is God's agent at work on the earth. Whenever God interacts with His creation it is through the Holy Spirit. When Jesus left the earth he said:

"But the Counselor, the Holy Spirit, whom the Father will send in my name, will teach you all things and will remind you of everything I have said to you."

John 14:26

The Holy Spirit is God and makes the Kingdom of God real to us. He makes Jesus real to us. He convicts us of sin, and points the way to the Savior. He moves powerfully to demonstrate the reality of God to us.

In the beginning of Creation, the Bible tells us that the earth was without form and void, and darkness was upon the face of the deep and the Spirit of God hovered on the face of the waters. Then God began to speak and things began to happen. As God spoke, the Holy Spirit began to do miraculous things, creating the earth and all we see, the birds, the trees, the fish and the animals.

The Holy Spirit is Almighty God. He is all powerful. Jesus was anointed by God the Holy Spirit, and when He performed a miracle it was by the power of the

Holy Spirit. The story of the woman with the issue of blood illustrates this reality:

> **And a woman was there who had been subject to bleeding for twelve years.**
>
> **She had suffered a great deal under the care of many doctors and had spent all she had, yet instead of getting better she grew worse.**
>
> **When she heard about Jesus, she came up behind him in the crowd and touched his cloak,**
>
> **because she thought, "If I just touch his clothes, I will be healed."**
>
> **Immediately her bleeding stopped and she felt in her body that she was freed from her suffering.**
>
> **At once Jesus realized that power had gone out from him. He turned around in the crowd and asked, "Who touched my clothes?"**
>
> **"You see the people crowding against you," his disciples answered, "and yet you can ask, 'Who touched me?'"**
>
> **But Jesus kept looking around to see who had done it.**
>
> **Then the woman, knowing what had happened to her, came and fell at his feet and, trembling with fear, told him the whole truth.**
>
> **He said to her, "Daughter, your faith has healed you. Go in peace and be freed from your suffering."**
>
> **Mark 5:25-34**

If you want healing you must recognize who Jesus is, and believe that as you reach out to Him for healing His power will be released. What was this power that left Jesus and healed this woman? It was the power of the Holy Spirit. At the commencement of His ministry Jesus said:

"The Spirit of the Lord is on me, because he has anointed me to preach good news to the poor. He has sent me to proclaim freedom for the prisoners and recovery of sight for the blind, to release the oppressed,

to proclaim the year of the Lord's favor."

Luke 4:18,19

This woman knew the Spirit of the Lord was upon Jesus. She knew the Holy Spirit of God would release this miracle because He had compassion on her.

The reason the power of Jesus could heal this woman was because He was endued with the power of the very Creator Himself. This power, the power of the Holy Spirit created this woman in the first place. It is no problem for God to correct and heal His creation.

One day as he was teaching, Pharisees and teachers of the law, who had come from every village of Galilee and from Judea and Jerusalem, were sitting there. And the power of the Lord was present for him to heal the sick.

Luke 5:17

The power of the Lord heals. The power of the Lord or the Holy Spirit is at work as you read this book. The power of Jesus is unlimited power. Jesus has power to calm storms, to walk on water, to raise the dead, to open blind eyes, to cleanse lepers and make the lame to walk. Jesus has power to heal you if you will only believe.

This woman had an illness no doctor could heal. She had this illness 12 years. She was desperate for a miracle to cure her. She had spent all the money she had trying to get healed. She was out of money, living in poverty. Not only had the medicine she had taken not cured her, but it had made her worse!

97

She was at the end of herself. She had tried every-thing humanly possible to be made well; and all the human methods of healing. No one or nothing could heal her. Only a miracle from God. Maybe you are read-ing this book and you have tried all the doctors and tried cures but nothing has worked. Maybe there is nothing that can cure you but a miracle from God. Reach out and believe Jesus to do the impossible in your life!

This was a woman who recognized who Jesus was. She recognized that He had the power to heal her disease. This recognition was faith — and as she reached out and touched the hem of Jesus' garment, power went out from Jesus. What was it that released the power that Jesus had? It was the faith of the woman. She had the faith to receive a miracle from him without even asking him.

Jesus was surrounded by a crowd of people and all of them would have been touching him, yet Jesus did not say "who touched me" when they touched Him. It was when a woman who had faith and determination, reached out and touched Him, believing and knowing He had power to heal, that power went out from Him. It was her faith, which Jesus recognized. Jesus responds to faith! If you reach out in faith to Jesus like this woman did, the power of the Holy Spirit will be released and you will be healed and receive your miracle from God.

Maybe you do not believe in Jesus or the Holy Spirit. I want to challenge you to consider my claims about Jesus. Perhaps if you reach out to Jesus like this woman did with all the faith you can muster, this power, this unlimited power will be released to heal your afflic-tion. The Holy Spirit works in the lives of people to bring them to relationship with God and to restore them spiritually, emotionally and physically.

In the book of John, the theme with respect to the Holy Spirit is new birth. Jesus said in John 3:3 that "I tell you the truth, no one can see the Kingdom of God unless he is born again." It is through the transforming work of the Holy Spirit that your life can be transformed. All the Holy Spirit is waiting for is an invitation.

I have ministered to many people who have no relationship with God and I came to the conclusion that the Holy Spirit is omnipresent and everywhere operative except for one place, the heart of the unbeliever. God will honor the free will of the human being and continue to seek ways to develop relationship with us, but He honors our rejection of Him.

Jesus said there are many sins which are forgivable, but one, that is the blasphemy or rejection of the Holy Spirit. We can sin and be forgiven of any sin, but the sin of rejection of the Holy Spirit cannot be forgiven by God because it is the one thing which a person needs in order to be born again.

The Holy Spirit is the person of the Trinity who communicates all the attributes of Christ to human beings. He is the new life that comes to live within people when they accept Christ as Savior. The Holy Spirit is one with God the Father and God the Son. Therefore, when we receive the Holy Spirit with the new birth experience, we receive God the Father and God the Son.

Luke's gospel and the book of Acts, emphasize the baptism in the Holy Spirit, which is a subsequent experience of empowerment. The new birth experience with the Holy Spirit produces the fruit of the Spirit, it represents who the Holy Spirit is. The new birth enables us to live as Jesus did and the baptism in the Holy Spirit gives us the power to do what Jesus did.

The Holy Spirit is real. Ask the Holy Spirit to come and touch your life and bring the reality of God to your life. The Holy Spirit will begin to work as soon as we invite Him to work. The Holy Spirit can show you so many things that no human being could never show you. Give Him a chance.

Chapter 11
The Voice of God and the Reality of God

M any think of God and hearing His voice as something, which is reserved for those who belong in
the insane asylum; but the Bible is full of people who
heard from God. God spoke to them and He is still speaking today. My first encounter with hearing the voice of
God was when I came to Christ.

I came to Christ through an evangelist who had
heard from God concerning me and my life. At that
time, all I wanted to do was know how this preacher had
heard what he heard. I wanted and needed to know that
it was God speaking. There was something about this
man hearing God's voice which fascinated me. I had
come from a church background which did not believe
you could hear God's voice directly, so this was interesting. Also this man had some knowledge concerning me
personally and my life which he could never have known
without prior knowledge of it. I knew instinctively it was
God speaking to me. I don't know how to explain it.

Since that time I have learned how to hear God's
voice for myself. There have been times when I didn't
know where to go or what to do and the voice of God has
directed me. I asked God once why He didn't speak in a
loud voice so everyone could hear, and I had the impres-

sion that God was saying that His voice was like the whisper of a lion. God does not need to prove anything to you or to me, He is God.

I shared earlier how God spoke to Moses from a burning bush and then sent him to deliver the children of Israel from the land of Egypt. Moses did everything God instructed and miracles began to happen. As God led the children of Israel into the wilderness, He supernaturally sustained them for 40 years with manna from heaven.

There is something about listening to the voice of God which unlocks the supernatural provision of God and the miracles of God. Jesus Himself was led and directed by the voice of God. God told the Children of Israel that He led them there to test them and to try them and to show them that man shall not live on bread alone, but by every word which proceeds from the mouth of God.

It was as these people listened to God that God took care of them. It is as we listen to God that He begins to move and act, and as our lives are directed by His voice He begins to take care of us supernaturally. Wherever Jesus went, He followed the direction of His heavenly Father and wherever He went miracles happened.

Many people have stories of how God spoke to them and when they listened they were protected supernaturally. God has our best interests in mind. He wants to take care of us and watch out for us. This ability that God can give to people, a supernatural knowledge that could only be known by God is another way God demonstrates His reality.

I have many friends, people in ministry and other walks of life, who have trusted God in similar ways and have seen God supernaturally sustain them. I have a friend who has six children. He felt God tell him to sell his house and everything he owned. Then he and his family began to travel the world praying for people in the nations and sharing the love of God.

When the money ran out, God began to supernaturally provide for them. They got back to the United States and someone offered to pay for him to go through Seminary. That is where I met him. He and his family have a vision to travel to Israel to minister in the Holy Land and all this time God has supernaturally sustained them. In my own life and ministry I have seen God supernaturally sustain what we have been doing as we have stepped out in faith and obedience to His leading.

There is a story in Scripture of Jesus walking on the water and Peter was in a boat and he called out, "Jesus, will you let me come to you," and Jesus said "yes." Peter did not step out of the boat onto the water, he stepped out on the word which came out of Jesus' mouth. This word supernaturally sustained him as he walked on water. There is something about hearing God's voice, which enables people to do the impossible.

I came to the United States to Oral Roberts University, because I felt God's leading to come, but I was also impressed with what one man had been able to do by listening to the voice of God and exercising faith. Oral Roberts shared that it was God who had spoken to Him about the University and it was as He followed God's instructions he was able to build it.

Noah built an Ark which God told him to build and it saved his family from destruction. God may be speaking to you today. He speaks to the human heart with a still small voice. He speaks to our conscience when we do something that is wrong. He speaks to us when we consider creation and all its wonders. He speaks in numerous ways. He is the God who spoke the universe into existence. He spoke you and I into existence. He is more than able to speak to you.

My prayer for you as you read this book is that you wouldn't harden your heart to what God is trying to speak to you, but that you would be open to what He has to say and listen quietly. God is speaking and like a radio that needs to be tuned into the right station to pick up the frequency we need to be tuned into God's station to hear what He is speaking to us. His frequency is another world, another realm, a Kingdom so beautiful it will take your breath away.

Chapter 12
The Bible, Miracles and the Reality of God

Whenever God does something to reveal Himself to human beings, a miracle occurs. Everything about God is supernatural and miraculous. If we say God is not supernatural and miraculous, we deny the very essence of who He is. The Bible is full of miracles. Let me list some of the greater and more well known miracles, those times where God met with people and revealed His glory.

Creation. God created everything we see out of nothing. The greatest supernatural miracle of all.

Noah and the Ark. God flooded the earth in judgment because of the wickedness of humanity and saved a remnant of humanity. Noah spent 100 years building an ark in obedience to God and God spared him and his family.

Abraham and the miracle child. Abraham was promised an heir to fulfill the promise that he would be the father of many nations, he waited 25 years for this child and his wife had a child when she was well past the age of child-bearing.

Joseph and his dream. God gave young Joseph a dream that he would be a great ruler. After experiencing much adversity, slavery and imprisonment he was promoted as ruler over Egypt.

Moses and the deliverance of the Children of Israel. God spoke to Moses in a burning bush and told him to challenge the Ruler of Egypt to free God's people. Many plagues were sent as God's sign that He was God and finally the children of Israel were delivered and walked through the Red Sea on dry land.

Supernatural feeding of the children of Israel. As they walked into the wilderness, God fed the children of Israel supernaturally. He fed them with angel's food, the bread of heaven so they might know that man does not live on bread alone, but by every word that proceeds from the mouth of God.

The taking of the land and the fall of Jericho. God had promised a good land to the children of Israel, but there were many obstacles in their way. Each time they sought God and His strategy they had a victory. The walls of Jericho, the first city, fell as they marched around the walls blowing trumpets.

Samson and destruction of Philistines. God put a great anointing for deliverance on Samson. He slew 1,000 men with the jawbone of a donkey.

David and Goliath. David slew the great giant Goliath with just a sling and a stone.

Elijah: Mt Carmel victory. Elijah called down fire from heaven to show all the people God was the true God.

Raising the widow's son. Elijah prayed for a widow's son and he came back to life.

The ravens feed Elijah. The land was in drought and God supernaturally fed Elijah who brought bread and meat to him morning and evening.

Elijah and the Chariot of fire. When Elijah was ready to leave the Earth a chariot of fire came from heaven and took him straight to heaven.

Elisha: The widow and cruise of oil. Elisha told the widow to take a jar of oil and fill as many jars as she could. As she filled the jars the oil did not run out.

Naaman's leprosy healed. A great Syrian general was healed of leprosy when Elisha told him to dip in the Jordan River seven times.

Esther and the salvation of the Jews. Esther and the Jews were threatened with a decree for the destruction of her people. She prayed and fasted and God intervened turning all the plans and schemes of her enemy against him to the point where he was hanged on his own gallows.

Job and the whirlwind. God stripped Job of everything he had and restored it seven fold back after a season of testing. God met Job and Job said, "before my ears had heard of you, but now my eyes have seen you."

Daniel and the Lion's den. Daniel was supernaturally saved from being eaten alive by lions.

Shadrach, Meshach, and Abed-nego. These three Hebrew children were saved from being burned alive in a furnace. They walked around in the midst of the fire unscathed.

Jonah and the whale. Jonah ran from his calling and God had him swallowed by a whale. He was spat up after three days outside the city he was called to, and the whole city repented.

Jesus: The virgin birth. Christ entered the world through the miracle of the virgin birth. Mary conceived by the Holy Spirit and God became flesh and lived among us.

Healing of the sick. Wherever Jesus went incredible miracles of healing accompanied his ministry. Mark 6:56 says as many as touched Him were made whole.

Feeding of the five thousand. Many people followed the ministry of Jesus, and there were times when He multiplied fish and bread and fed thousands of them.

Walking on water. Jesus walked on water to prove that when you walk in the Kingdom you can defy the laws of gravity to achieve Kingdom purposes.

Crucifixion and resurrection. Jesus was crucified as a sacrifice for the sin of humanity. He rose from the grave after three days, demonstrating His power over sin, death and all forms of evil.

Jesus appears to many. After His resurrection Christ appears to many over a period of forty days.

The ascension. Jesus ascended into heaven as they all watched.

The outpouring at Pentecost. Jesus formed His Church with a mighty outpouring of Holy Spirit power that launched the Church from being hidden, shy and undercover, to being bold proclaimers of the risen Christ.

With each of these miracles, God is revealing Himself as a supernatural God. God's interactions with human beings are always supernatural. We should expect the supernatural to happen when we encounter God. God just can't help Himself — it's who He is. God is supernatural. Miracles are normal for God. Sometimes His miracles are to reveal Himself, others to show His compassion, others to demonstrate His power.

It seems with some of these circumstances God allowed them to happen so that the glory of God might be revealed in greater ways. I call these circumstances situations of impossibility. For example, the deliverance of the children of Israel at the Red Sea crossing, where God led His people to a place which looked impossible. They had the sea in front of them and a hostile army behind them and yet God had promised them they would be free. In order for God's Word to be true, a miracle had to happen. There was no other way these people could have been free.

Their situation was impossible, and in many respects it was not a situation which was their doing. God had led them to an impossible place for a reason. He wanted to be glorified. Many times God wants people to see He is real, so He allows situations of impossibility to demonstrate His reality.

Maybe you are facing an impossible situation in your life. Maybe you say I will never meet God, it is impossible. God may have allowed you to reach this place in order to show up in your life, to reveal His glory to you, to reveal His reality to you.

I want to share with you a story from the Bible concerning the great prophet Elijah which illustrates the supernatural ability of God. It is found in First Kings 17. Elijah is sent by God to a brook and there is a famine in the land. God says to him in verse four, "And it will be that you shall drink from the brook, and I have commanded the ravens to feed you there."

We all know this is an impossibility — ravens do not feed people, but when God said it would be, it was. In verse six we read: "The ravens brought him bread and meat in the morning and bread and meat in the evening, and he drank from the brook."

Even when "our" reality says, nothing is going to happen and when we see no way forward, we see nothing in our reality which would indicate that we can make it or survive, God speaks and things change, things happen.

God spoke to the ravens and the ravens were instantly transformed from being scavengers of death to givers of life. Jesus spoke to the storms and the storms obeyed. We need to understand that God's reality is different to our reality.

Consider also with me a story from the Gospel of Luke 8:49-55:

> While Jesus was still speaking, someone came from the house of Jairus, the synagogue ruler. "Your daughter is dead," he said. "Don't bother the teacher any more."
>
> Hearing this, Jesus said to Jairus, "Don't be afraid; just believe, and she will be healed."
>
> When Jesus arrived at the house of Jairus, he did not let anyone go in with him except Peter, John and James, and the child's father and mother.
>
> Meanwhile, all the people were wailing and mourning for her. "Stop wailing," Jesus said. "She is not dead but asleep."
>
> They laughed at him, knowing that she was dead.
>
> But he took her by the hand and said, "My child, get up!"
>
> Her spirit returned, and at once she stood up. Then Jesus told them to give her something to eat.

When the synagogue ruler came to Jesus, he came to him with an entirely impossible situation. His daughter was dead. This man was heart broken and came to Jesus in desperation. He had heard of Jesus and thought maybe Jesus, in all His unlimited power, could do something for him. Jesus' response was different to what we would expect. He said: "Don't be afraid; just believe, and she will be healed," and then He says, "She is not dead but asleep!"

Why did Jesus say these incredible and seemingly impossible things? The people laughed at him, He was saying things from His perspective. They thought He was a crazy man, but they had no idea who they were dealing with. They were dealing with the very Creator of the universe, who saw things differently.

The Bible says, "with God all things are possible." To Jesus the girl was asleep. To everyone else she was dead. We need to have this same perspective as Jesus. If you are faced with an impossible situation, you need to understand God does not see it as a problem. With Him all things are possible. You need to have God's perspective.

Jesus put out of the room everyone who was mourning and who did not believe He could do this miracle. Those who did not have His perspective of the situation. Those who did not understand what He was capable of doing. Sometimes if you want a miracle from God, you need to put away and ignore all those who do not have God's perspective. Those who do not believe that with God all things are possible. You need to put them out of your life and say, "God I believe with you all things are possible." For you this problem is nothing.

Maybe you are faced with a situation, which to you seems humanly impossible to fix. The truth is it probably is humanly impossible to fix. Maybe you are looking at this mountain and like these people in your unbelief you are wailing and crying. Jesus does not see your problem the way you do. He would say, "why are you looking at these things. I can take care of them easily. With Me all things are possible." Jesus laughs at impossible situations. He walks on water and calms the storms with a Word of His power.

The reality of God is different from the reality we have come to know. Our reality is defined by the notion that unless we can see it or touch it or feel it does not exist. Our reality is defined by the age of the enlighten-ment and the philosophies of our day.

I remember when I met God I thought to myself, there was no faith involved in this. I had seen God and experienced Him in spite of my unbelief. I wanted God to make Himself real to me and He had done it. I had not taken a leap of faith, God had leaped across the gap between us and introduced Himself.

I am under the firm conviction that God is real whether we believe it or not. He is more concrete than concrete. He is more alive than we are alive. God is real. What does that mean? It means that He is watching you now as you read this book. He hears your thoughts, He sees your heart. He knows what you are thinking about. There are a huge amount of implications to the reality of God. Not only is He real but He wants to meet with you.

Many of us believe that people need to have faith to believe that God exists. They say that God is invisible and you can experience Him, but you need to have faith that He is there. I believe this puts too much on the indi-vidual. The Bible tells us that no one can come to God unless the Spirit of God draws them. Everything starts with God. He is watching you as you read this book. He is always thinking about you and looking for ways to communicate with you.

Chapter 13
Sin, the Devil, and the Reality of God

Many people in our society relegate Christianity and its notions of good, evil and sin as being relics of a bygone era. What we like to think is that people are basically good and that if there is an evil it is really only a by product of a society which is not adequately taking care of its own.

We say that people commit crime because they come from an impoverished background. They are victims of circumstance. I'm not sure this argument explains the crime that is committed by those who come from a wealthy background. What is this predisposition towards evil in the human race?

Sin, the human condition and evil has occupied the thoughts of scholars and philosophers throughout history. Before considering the biblical perspective, let's consider some of the differing views of sin and the human condition. The New Age movement and movements with a similar ideological framework, refuse to acknowledge sin at all, holding the belief that people are essentially good with the capacity to do evil.

Other naturalistic belief systems hold a view of humans that regards them as essentially evolved creatures and that therefore there is no way of defining sin. These systems argue that society may have agreed certain laws regulate errant human behavior, but that there is no absolute truth.

Essentially many of the modern forms of thought for various reasons refuse to acknowledge sin in much the same way as they refuse to acknowledge God. Because they refuse to acknowledge God, they feel they can escape the need to be accountable to God. Unfortunately whether they like it or not, God does exist and will require each human being to give an account for his or her life on the day of judgment (2 Corinthians 5:10).

With respect to the biblical view, Cornelius Van Til defines sin as "any want of or lack of conformity to the law of God."[36] It is humanity's conformity, or lack thereof to God's standard of holiness and righteousness that defines sin. Others define sin or the essence of sin as the failure to acknowledge God as God.[37]

There are many differing definitions of sin. Erickson uses a number of words to define sin, these are: Missing the mark, irreligion, transgression, iniquity or lack of integrity, rebellion, treachery, perversion, and abomination.[38]

These words and definitions provide us with concepts, which on the surface consider the actions of a person before God. It is critical to consider therefore, the deeper issues of the actual state or condition of a person before God.

The issue of why a person sins or why people commit evil acts lies at the heart of the human condition. As mentioned previously, many with a naturalistic worldview believe there is no real existence of sin or God, however there are naturalistic theories which do try to explain the human condition and its tendency to commit evil acts.

Pfleiderer argues that humans like all creatures are driven to satisfy their own natural impulses, which are not necessarily evil or sinful. As humans advanced and developed higher laws, a conflict arose. Pfleiderer argues that the attempt to bring the natural impulses into alignment with the higher laws results in the occasion for sin. [39]

Niebuhr sees the human condition as being the struggle between humanity's finite aspects on the one hand and infinite aspirations on the other. This conflict between these two aspects results in an anxiety, which produces the occasion of sin. To overcome this anxiety, humans will engage in forms of sensuality or pride.

There are a number of other views on the condition of humanity leading to the occasion for sin. Pascal argues humans are notoriously inconsistent and bored and this is what leads to sin. As mentioned earlier, others have sought to trace sin to social and economic struggles. [40] The Bible details in the book of Genesis very clearly, what the source of the human predisposition to sin is, and therefore what it is that causes people to sin.

When God created Adam and Eve, He created perfect creatures made in His image and likeness (Genesis 1:26). He gave them the charge to be fruitful, multiply, replenish the earth and have dominion over it (Genesis 1:28). He stipulated in Genesis 2:17 that "but you must not eat from the tree of the knowledge of good and evil, for when you eat of it you shall surely die."

The serpent deceived the woman into eating the fruit of the tree and it was at that point through an act of disobedience that their condition changed (Genesis 3:6,7). It was possibly a combination of eating the fruit and the disobedience of the act, which caused the fall and their change in nature. The tragedy of the fall then occurred and God pronounced judgment on them and removed them from the Garden of Eden (Genesis 3:13-24).

The fall of the condition of these humans resulted in an immediate spiritual death, a deferred physical death and a second death of final judgment.[41] In addition to death, their innocence was lost, their fellowship with God was broken and their nature became infected with the disease of sin. This fallen human condition was passed on to successive generations and we see the initial effects of this fallen condition in successive generations in Cain's murder of his brother.

There are a number of theories with respect to the doctrine of original or inherited sin. Pelagians do not agree that sin is inherited, but that each new person has a clean slate at birth and at some point in their life make the choice to sin. I believe in traducianism, which argues that both our spiritual and our physical natures are inherited from our parents.

Whatever view one holds it seems clear from scripture that humans are not sinners only because of their sinful actions, but also because they are inherently sinful in their nature. Original inherited sin assumes that from birth a person is born in sin and separated from God. I hold the view however, that it is not until a child reaches the age of accountability, which is determined by God, that the guilt for that sinful condition is effective. If a child died before the age of accountability, he would go to heaven. This view holds that a person inherits sin; but not the corresponding guilt for that sin.[42]

In this world we see many evil things. In the news, we constantly see the acts of humanity, which cause so much pain and suffering to others. God hates sin because it causes suffering. He hates adultery, murder, theft and all the sins of humanity because of the pain caused to others. Jesus said if we obeyed the commandment to love God and love others we would never sin. Sin is essentially hatred toward others and God.

Many see God as someone who has a list of do's and don'ts and someone who wants to spoil their fun. Much of what people do to satisfy their craving for lust or revenge causes tremendous amounts of pain to others. Jesus calls us to love and forgiveness because it is the way to end suffering. He calls us to turn from sin and receive His forgiveness and salvation because it is the way to bring an end to the suffering of humanity.

When Jesus came to the earth, much of His teaching addressed the issue of the heart. He taught that to hate someone was the same as murder, because it is in the heart that the sin begins. Jesus knew the problems of humanity needed to be addressed at their source. It's not just what we do that God watches, He looks at the thoughts and intentions of our heart. If God can change your heart, your whole life can be changed.

In addition to the evil caused by the evil actions and sin of humanity, I want to argue the case for the existence of an evil force at work in this world which has pervaded society and is at work to destroy people.

The thief comes only to steal and kill and destroy; I have come that they may have life, and have it to the full.
John 10:10

The Bible also tells us that:

The god of this age has blinded the minds of unbelievers, so that they cannot see the light of the gospel of the glory of Christ, who is the image of God.
2 Corinthians 4:4

If you are reading this book, I am praying that God will allow your eyes to be opened. There are forces at work trying to stop you believing in God even now. There is a great spiritual battle for your soul. The devil wants your soul. Whether or not you believe it, you are in a spiritual battle.

Human beings have a spiritual hunger, which must be satisfied, and because the Church has not adequately addressed this issue, people are looking to involve themselves in activities, which involve spiritual elements.

People will go to fortune tellers to have their fortunes told, they will dabble with the occult trying to communicate with the dead, they will experiment with different forms of witchcraft and occult practices. Many who have tried these things can attest to the fact that there are real forces at work, forces that cannot be explained in natural terms.

In recent years, we see the number of movies with paranormal themes have risen dramatically. Why is there such an increase in interest in paranormal topics? Filmmakers didn't create this interest, they merely cash in on it. The interest existed before these films were ever created. So what is responsible for the underlying interest in paranormal subject matter?

Jeffrey Palmer, a secular commentator addresses this issue and states: "Perhaps there is disillusionment with modern society that leads many to explore paranormal ideas and concepts. Many mainstream beliefs and practices have left a large section of the population feeling disappointed and confused.

Organized religion provides a clue into the disillusionment with modern beliefs that may be responsible for the upswing in interest into paranormal subjects. The

Catholic Church, for one, has suffered a huge amount of negative publicity surrounding the abuse scandals of several priests.

Other religious doctrines seem to be losing credibility or at least generating less interest than they once enjoyed. Many people are seeking a personalized form of spirituality that moves away from institutionalized doctrines and dogmas and focuses more on the discovery of the spiritual self.

Modern science brings another plate to the interest in the paranormal topics table. Today physicists are publishing scientific articles and research that seems to validate many age old mystical and esoteric concepts. String theory physicists talk about the existence of a multi-dimensional universe. Scientists have successfully demonstrated the ability of a single photon of light to exist simultaneously in two separate places. More and more the study of physics moves into the realm of the paranormal, with strange and fascinating results.

Disillusionment with antiquated beliefs as well as modern society, the real need to discover a personal sense of spirituality and the validation of mystical concepts by modern scientists, may be responsible for the increasing interest in paranormal subject matter. We see this interest reflected in the cinemas, on television, on the book shelves and on the radio. Every media outlet is aware of this trend and there seems to be a rush to produce as many products as possible."[43]

There is a hunger in the human heart for the supernatural! This is a God-given hunger! Western society and communist countries have literally starved citizens of anything spiritual and now people are crying out to have this hunger satisfied.

Maybe today you are crying out — what is this void that I have in my soul? Let God hear your cry. Ask Jesus Christ to come to you and make Himself real to you like He did to doubting Thomas. God is real and He will make Himself real to you!

What will it take to convince you of the reality of God? Why don't you to share whatever is on your heart with Him. Now is your chance to meet with and encounter God. Maybe you have read this book and you have a deep hunger within you, which just will not go away. You have tried everything to fill it but it will not go away. God knows about your hunger and He wants to fill it. Let Him come and make Himself real to you.

Chapter 14
The Upside Down Kingdom and the Reality of God

God and His Kingdom function in almost the opposite way to the way we are accustomed to in our world. Our world is upside down compared to the Kingdom of God. Everything operates differently in the Kingdom of God. Our world in comparison to God's Kingdom is an ugly place. God's Kingdom is a beautiful realm, where ugliness has no place. Sure there are things in our world which are beautiful, but they do not compare to the beauty of the Kingdom of God.

The ugliness in our world stems from the problems of sin and evil. The whole world is marred by the curse, which came upon humanity at the fall. Unless you see the beauty of God's Kingdom, you can never fully comprehend how ugly and unreal this world is. An encounter with God will transform the way you see things.

In our world, everyone is focused on themselves and what they can get out of life. They are focused on their life and how they can have a better life. There is a selfishness which is inherent in human nature. If there is conflict, they get even, they get justice quickly and at any cost.

The world has a certain way of operating, its leaders exercise authority over their subjects, they deal with the issues of society through political maneuvering. They believe that if they can remove poverty they can remove crime. Their policies reflect their belief that the problems of humanity are surface level; but the problems of humanity are deeper than what these political policies indicate. Humanity needs a heart transplant, a life transforming encounter with the Living God. Jesus came to bring that kind of change.

Two thousand years ago Jesus Christ came to this earth and at the end of His life He was crucified on a criminal's cross. Just before He was crucified, Pontius Pilate asked Him the question:

> **Pilate then went back inside the palace, summoned Jesus and asked him, "Are you the king of the Jews?"**
>
> **"Is that your own idea," Jesus asked, "or did others talk to you about me?"**
>
> **"Am I a Jew?" Pilate replied. "It was your people and your chief priests who handed you over to me. What is it you have done?"**
>
> **Jesus said, "My kingdom is not of this world. If it were, my servants would fight to prevent my arrest by the Jews. But now my kingdom is from another place."**
>
> **John 18:33-36**

What is Jesus saying here? I believe He is talking about another reality which is greater than the one we live in. Jesus' Kingdom is a Kingdom which brings change to the human heart. Those who enter this Kingdom and are part of it, live differently to others. They have new natures and they live by a different set of standards.

Jesus came to bring a revolution to the world. He taught that those in His Kingdom should love their enemies, bless those who curse them and pray for those who despitefully use them and persecute them. He taught that if someone strikes us on one cheek we should turn the other cheek and that if someone asks for our coat we should give them our cloak also, that if someone asks us to go one mile with them we should go another mile. This kind of thinking is crazy in our world. Our response to someone who injures us is, 'why should I forgive that person they hurt me or they insulted me?' and we harbor unforgiveness and bitterness towards them. If someone hits us we want to strike back and protect ourselves.

Jesus' Kingdom is not a Kingdom of hate, but one of love. The Bible tells us that God is love and those who are part of His Kingdom would be known by the love they have for one another. In our world we see unforgiveness, bitterness, envy and anger, hatred, violence and all forms of emotion and action which represent the unwillingness of humanity to love and forgive. It is, as we make the decision to love and forgive, that we can start to see something which could bring change to this world.

Although Mahatma Gandhi was not a Christian, he applied the principles of the Kingdom of God to great effect in Indian Society. He invoked a revolution by applying the teachings of Christ and removed the whole nation of India from an oppressive form of government through non-violent means. He did not accept Christ was Savior, but his application of Christ's principles changed the course of his nation's history.

Gandhi said, "when I despair, I remember that all through history the ways of truth and love have always won. There have been tyrants, and murderers, and for a time they can seem invincible, but in the end they always fall. Think of it always."[44] Gandhi did not accept the Deity of Christ and His redemptive work at the cross, but he did understand that held within the teachings of

Christ — the principles of the Kingdom of God, the answers to the problems of humanity could be found.

There have been many tyrants throughout history who have shown us how far the depths of human depravity can extend. The levels of evil and atrocity that human beings are able to inflict upon one another is truly astounding. The world was shocked at the discovery of the Nazi death camps at the end of the second world war, the various mass slaughter and genocides that have occurred in the nations throughout the centuries. The brutality of the treatment that one group have been able to inflict upon another group shows us what can happen in a world without love.

Yet in the midst of these atrocities there were those whose lives continued to shine in the midst of the darkness. There are many stories of those who helped the Jewish people during the second world war. One of these was Corrie Ten Boom, a Christian woman who sheltered and protected Jewish people from the death camps. Eventually her and her family were caught and sent to a camp as well. She was subjected to the brutal treatment of the Nazi soldiers. She had the kind of faith that enabled her to forgive these prison guards. From the depths of a Nazi death camp she said, "No matter how deep our darkness, God's love is deeper still."[45]

I have a friend who has traveled the world, carrying a large wooden cross, sharing the love of Jesus with people on the streets. He has traveled through many war torn nations and as he has carried the cross, that symbol of God's love and forgiveness for humanity, he said that he had concluded that all the conflict in the world is caused by unforgiveness.

Martin Luther King Jr. understood this truth and he applied the principles of the Kingdom of God to effect change in segregated America. Martin Luther King Jr. brought the revolutionary concepts of Christ to bear on the problems he faced in his generation. He said in one of his rousing speeches "darkness cannot drive out darkness; only light can do that. Hate cannot drive out hate; only love can do that. Hate multiplies hate, violence multiplies violence, and toughness multiplies toughness in a descending spiral of destruction....The chain reaction of evil — hate begetting hate, wars producing more wars — must be broken, or we shall be plunged into the dark abyss of annihilation."[46]

Martin Luther King understood that the buck needed to stop somewhere, that hate multiplies hate and only a response of love and forgiveness can stop it. Love cancels out hate. Forgiveness and love are the only weapons which defeat hatred and unforgiveness. This is what Jesus taught. The principles of the Kingdom of God work!

There are many wonderful Christians we can look to who have applied the principles of the Kingdom to produce revolution and change. William Wilberforce challenged the evils of the slave trade in his day. His tireless work in the political realms eventually brought an end to the slave trade. He believed that the treatment of slaves was contrary to the teachings of scripture and the teachings of Christ.

Wilberforce said, "Is it not the great end of religion, and, in particular, the glory of Christianity, to extinguish the malignant passions; to curb the violence, to control the appetites, and to smooth the asperities of man; to make us compassionate and kind, and forgiving one to another; to make us good husbands, good fathers, good friends; and to render us active and useful in the discharge of the relative social and civil duties?"[47]

Wilberforce understood that the key to fixing the problems of humanity and society was a change in the human heart, which was brought about through relationship with God. His relationship with Christ gave him the determination to bring an end to the slave trade. He commented, "So enormous, so dreadful, so irremediable did the trade's wickedness appear that my own mind was completely made up for abolition. Let the consequences be what they would, I from this time determined that I would never rest until I had effected its abolition."[48]

Christ taught that we should show compassion for the poor. Christ taught the parable of the good Samaritan and the need to show love and care to those more disadvantaged than us. Mother Theresa is a wonderful example to us of the compassion of Christ and the love of Christ for a suffering humanity. Her work was done with love and with so little financial support. She has shown the world what change, a person with the simple compassion of Christ, can bring.

Many of the self help books we read, the motivational or books with success principles use the principles of the Kingdom of God. The principles of the Kingdom are to be used in their truest form in the context of relationship with God and for the glory of God, however, many use them to benefit themselves.

Even when used for selfish purposes these principles work. They are like the law of gravity which God has put in place, they operate, they have been set in place by God. We can't see the law of gravity, however we know it exists. When we respect the law of gravity things go well for us. We don't jump off tall buildings because we respect the law of gravity. If we don't we will get hurt.

People who apply the principles of the Kingdom lead happier, more successful lives. People who don't,

126

typically lead unhappy lives and do injury to themselves and to others. Sadly, many of those who use the principles of the Kingdom of God are missing the relationship with the Giver of the principles.

I remember a number of years ago talking with a Korean business student about the claims of Christianity. He said Christianity interested him and he had been reading a book with success principles based on the teachings of Christ. I said to him, "have you ever thanked Christ for the principles? Have you ever thanked God for giving you the principles?" He looked at me with a stunned look in His face. He had never even considered this possibility. He was using the principles of the King of the Kingdom and getting benefit from them, but he had never stopped to thank the King.

Maybe that is you today as you read this book. You have based your life on a number of principles which are based on the teachings of Christ and you have been experiencing a measure of success in your life due to the use of these principles. You could start by thanking Christ for the principles you are using and ask Him to make Himself real to you. Start a friendship and a relationship with the Giver of your success principles! God wants you to be happy in this life, believe me, but the greatest sense of happiness you will ever have is when you encounter the source of all happiness.

I remember as a young Christian and being in prayer with some friends and an overwhelming sense of God's presence filled the room and all of us began to laugh uncontrollably. We were experiencing the source of all happiness and joy. The Bible tells in God's presence there is fullness of joy. You can experience many things in life which provide happiness and joy, but there is nothing like being in the presence of God.

I was visiting New Zealand a few years ago and had been traveling the world seeing all the sights of Europe, living a luxurious lifestyle. I was sitting in the living room of an evangelist. His family were all exited to hear about where I had been and what I done. While we were there, the evangelist prayed for my friend and I felt a tremendous sense of God's presence.

Here I was, I had traveled the world, lived in the finest places, eaten in the finest restaurants and I was sitting in a humble family living room, on the outskirts of Auckland in New Zealand, on the edge of the world. I felt so happy and content in that moment. I thought there was no place I would rather be in that moment than in the presence of God. I had everything I could ever need and had done all the glamorous things I could have done, but nothing compared to that moment. It was a humble place, but I would have gladly traded all the previous experiences for that moment in the presence of God.

I imagine it must be how the three wise men felt when they went to visit the humble birthplace of Jesus. These were men who had the wealth of the East at their disposal, and here they were, everyone probably wondered why they were there. They were in a little, unknown town in Israel, visiting a stable, spending their time with humble people; people who took care of sheep for a living.

Yet these men knew there are some things in life which are more precious than gold, that are worth more than the most costly fragrances, more than all the money in the world could buy. They were there experiencing something greater than they could probably express. The birth of the Savior of the world. Christ came into this world as God's gift to humanity. Why not consider coming to God to ask Him for that free gift which is the

128

most precious commodity in the universe? The thing which cost God everything costs you nothing, the gift of salvation and eternal life through Jesus Christ.

The principle "do unto others as you would have them do unto you" is the golden rule. There are many religions which adhere to this principle. It is a universal principle taught in many religions and many cultures, but there is something about this principle which teaches us about the heart of the Kingdom of God. In the Kingdom there is a humble consideration of the needs of others, there is a love for others that goes deeper than anything many of us have ever experienced. The heart of the Kingdom is a self sacrificial love, a love which we see demonstrated by Christ as He went to the cross for humanity.

Even before you knew Christ, He made His sacrifice for you. Maybe you are reading this book and you don't know Christ — Jesus Christ has made His sacrifice for you. He made it in advance for you and me, knowing we would need what He did. He did it knowing we would live our own way, with no knowledge of God and would possibly even never know Him, and yet He paid the price in full.

In the midst of our ignorance, Christ sacrificed His life for us. We ignore God and pretend He doesn't exist. While we carry on with our lives and live whatever way we choose, He came and suffered and died, yet many do not know Him. Even when we choose to ignore Him, God extends His love towards us. It is His love which is crying out to you this very moment. It is the Kingdom of God.

When someone is willing to suffer and die for you, you know that is love. In this world it's everyone for themselves, but when it comes to the ones we love we are more prepared to do things to protect them and to make sacrifices in order to ensure their happiness and well-being. This world is God's family — He is the Father of Creation and He made that decision out of love for His lost children. He would do anything to ensure their happiness and well-being. The greatest happiness we can know is through relationship with God.

Jesus' Kingdom seeks to resolve the problems of the world by dealing with the issues of the heart. It deals with the spiritual problems behind the physical problems. His Kingdom deals with the issue of sin. He died, He laid His life down as payment for our sin, we can have forgiveness of our sins through this Kingdom. It is only when the problem of sin in the human heart is solved, that the problems of this world will be solved. God's focus is on your heart. He wants to change it and make you a new creation.

The Kingdom of God is a Kingdom of the heart. I remember being in London when Princess Diana died, and the whole nation came to a complete standstill. The streets were lined with flowers and there was a deluge of flowers outside the grounds of Buckingham Palace. Princess Diana was the people's princess.

I remember watching a documentary on her life and a journalist asked her what kind of queen she would be.

Diana replied, "I don't want to be a normal queen, in a formal official sense. If I am to be a queen, I want to be known as a queen of the heart." Princess Diana understood that the key to people was the heart. She won the hearts of the people and her death brought the nation of Britain and the nations of the entire world to a standstill.

Everything springs from the heart. Jesus knew this secret and He targeted the hearts of human beings to bring His Kingdom to Earth. Jesus came into this world in such a humble way, humbling Himself to go to the cross for humanity seeking to win the human heart.

When the movie *The Passion of the Christ* was released, many came to view the movie and were struck and impacted in many ways by what Christ was prepared to do to win the human heart. They were struck with the brutality He was prepared to suffer on behalf of a hurting world. They were struck with what He was prepared to do to bring change, and they were struck with the humility He showed as He walked to the Cross like a lamb led to the slaughter. Two thousand years after His life on the Earth and His death, Christ is still impacting human hearts.

Our decisions are made with the heart. The Bible warns us to guard our heart "because out of the heart flow the issues of life." If your heart is full of the love of God and the Holy Spirit, then your life will be changed and you will be a member of God's Kingdom. If you have the Holy Spirit in your heart, then your life will be influenced towards godliness, holiness and righteousness. Jesus' Kingdom is a Kingdom of the heart. Maybe as you read this book your heart is being moved by Jesus. I want to encourage you to invite the Holy Spirit to come into your heart and bring change.

This Kingdom of God brings new life, through faith in Christ we can be spiritually born again. This issue was addressed by Jesus when Nicodemus, the Pharisee and respected elder, came to Jesus by night and asked Him about the Kingdom of God. Jesus had this to say in John 3:1-8:

Now there was a man of the Pharisees named Nicodemus, a member of the Jewish ruling council.

He came to Jesus at night and said, "Rabbi, we know you are a teacher who has come from God. For no one could perform the miraculous signs you are doing if God were not with him."

In reply Jesus declared, "I tell you the truth, no one can see the kingdom of God unless he is born again."

"How can a man be born when he is old?" Nicodemus asked. "Surely he cannot enter a second time into his mother's womb to be born!"

Jesus answered, "I tell you the truth, no one can enter the kingdom of God unless he is born of water and the Spirit.

Flesh gives birth to flesh, but the Spirit gives birth to spirit.

You should not be surprised at my saying, 'You must be born again.'

The wind blows wherever it pleases. You hear its sound, but you cannot tell where it comes from or where it is going. So it is with everyone born of the Spirit."

In order to enter God's Kingdom it is critical to have a new spiritual birth, become a new creature, transformed and renewed. The Holy Spirit comes into the heart and brings cleansing and change. He brings life where there is spiritual death. At the time of new birth, you enter into a new Kingdom, a new reality, a new dimension where everything changes and new principles apply. As a citizen of this new Kingdom there is a desire within you to want to participate in the dynamics of this new Kingdom.

The Kingdom of God brings healing to those who are sick. Sickness came to humanity as a result of the fall. In this Kingdom there is no sickness. The Kingdom repairs all the damage which has been wrought by the enemy's kingdom.

Jesus lived His life to bring healing to the sick, sight to the blind and to relieve the oppressed. He went about doing good, healing all who were sick and oppressed of the devil for God was with Him. He came to heal the broken hearted and to bind up their wounds. He died to redeem humanity. Everything He did was driven by the love and compassion of God for a world separated from God, a world full of suffering.

Many of us know the Scripture in John 3:16,17:

"For God so loved the world that he gave his one and only Son, that whoever believes in him shall not perish but have eternal life.

For God did not send his Son into the world to condemn the world, but to save the world through him."

Jesus was God in the flesh and His mission was compassion for humanity. God loved you so much He sent His only Son, to come and to suffer and to die in your place. This is the kind of God who is not distant, not unconcerned with the affairs of our lives, but is more deeply committed to us than we can possibly imagine.

Just before He was crucified, Jesus spent time washing His disciples' feet, an act which would normally be undertaken by servants, but Jesus showed them that in His Kingdom, the greatest was the servant of all. What an upside down concept! That the God of the universe should humble Himself and serve others as a model for leadership and greatness is a strange concept.

The concept that the God who created everything could demonstrate humility and servanthood runs counter to our understanding. Jesus came to this world, He was born in a manger in a lowly stable. He lived His life with simplicity, not pomp and grandeur, then He died on a cross between two criminals.

The road to the cross was also marked with humility. Jesus said to God, "not my will but your will be done." He went to the cross and as people falsely accused Him, He offered no response. It was this road of lowliness and humility that brought a new Kingdom into this world.

Jesus said, "come to me all you who are weary and heavy laden I will give you rest. Take My yoke upon you for I am meek and lowly of heart and you will find rest for your souls. God is humble, what an amazing concept! The fact that God is humble still astounds me. He has no reason to be and yet this is His nature. How many rulers throughout history have promoted humility and servant-hood as virtues? This is what Jesus and His Kingdom are all about.

Jesus taught things like, "give and it shall be given unto you." This is opposite to the way it is in the world. In our world we take what we can get, it's every man for himself. Ultimately in the Kingdom of God there is love. Love for God and love for others. In the Kingdom of God everything centers on God and not on us. Those in this world live to see how much they can get out of this life for themselves, but in the Kingdom of God, there is a selflessness, a desire to serve others.

In the Kingdom of God people and relationship with God are more important than material things. Many of those who have had all that life can offer can attest to the fact that material things do not bring happiness. Ultimately it is relationship with God and others that bring happiness. Jesus taught that material things are what the world runs after, but His view was "seek first the Kingdom of God and all these things shall be added unto you" (Matthew 6:33).

Chapter 15
Let Me Pray for You

In the final analysis, none of what I have shared can make God suddenly appear to you. It's not like rubbing a magic bottle to get a genie to appear. I can't make God appear for my next party trick. God is God, I am not, but I'm pointing you in His direction. I'm saying to you, it is possible to have an encounter with Him. If He can do it for me, believe me, He can do it for you. I was the ultimate doubting Thomas. I know God has compassion and a heart for the doubting Thomas's of this world. That means He has His eye on you my friend.

I want to ask you to consider that while you may have been looking for a sign from God, something to prove to you that He is real, that maybe God is looking for a sign from you, maybe He is looking for an open door. Maybe you have to open up your heart and mind to the possibility that He exists and to the possibility that you can meet with Him. Communication is a two way street, as we all know.

I also want to take a moment to manage expectations. Even if you make the decision to be open to God, don't expect an instantaneous response, although that may happen. Allow God to be God and reveal Himself to you in the way He chooses and at the time He chooses. Be assured that if you keep that door open, God will come to you and knock, and when He does, He will make Himself real to you.

If you do open up to God, I want to encourage you not to be too specific concerning your requirements. Don't ask God to jump through too many hoops. God knows what it will take for you to be convinced. He is just looking for an opportunity, for an open door.

I want to pray a prayer for you as you read this book. Whether you believe anything I have said or not, allow me to pray this prayer for you, please.

"God, You are the answer to all our questions. You are the fulfillment of every promise, You are the miracle we need. I pray for the person reading this book. I know You don't need me to defend You. I know You don't need any help from me to prove Yourself to this person. I'm asking You to prove Yourself beyond a shadow of doubt that You exist. God, do whatever it takes to reveal to them how beautiful You truly are. Reveal Yourself in the beauty of Your holiness. Appear to this person, like You did to Thomas, Jesus. Appear to them like You did to me. Show them You are alive. Show them how much you love them, that You died in their place, even if they have no idea who You are. God I pray for a miracle in Jesus' Name."

Maybe you are more adventurous and you are ready for commitment to Christ now. As you have read this book, you are convinced enough now and you want to make a commitment right now based on what you have seen and heard. God wants you to ask Him to forgive your sin, God wants you to ask the Holy Spirit to come into your heart and life and He wants you to confess Jesus Christ as Savior and Lord. He wants you to be His child to have relationship with Him.

I suggest you pray a prayer to God similar to this one. Make sure whatever you pray, you mean it and you are being real with God.

"God, I thank You that You are real, and that I know You are there. I'm ready to develop a relationship with You. I come to You right now, just the way I am. I know I am not perfect and that in my life there are many things I have done which are not pleasing to You. There is sin in my life. I know You are a holy God and I ask You to forgive my sin, and that You cover my sin with the blood of Your Son Jesus. Jesus, I thank You for dying for me on the cross. I thank You for what You did to save me and I receive You as my Savior this very moment. Holy Spirit, I invite You into my heart and life, I invite You to come and make me a new creature in Christ. Father God, I thank You that now I am Your child. I thank You that nothing can separate me from Your love, that I am Your child forever."

I want to say at this point that if you have prayed this prayer, and you have felt something change in your heart and life, here are some suggestions. Firstly, I would encourage you to get a hold of the Bible and begin to read the gospel of John. This is a great book to get an understanding of the basics of the Gospel and what Christ came to do. It's important for you to spend time reading the Word of God.

I would also encourage you to constantly commune with God. Not in a religious way, don't make it a ritual, but spend time as you would with someone you love. Treasure the time you spend with God. Spend as much time as you can with Him. Even when you're at work, involve God in everything. Allow Him to be a part of your life.

I would encourage you to ask God to show you a good Church to attend. Find a good pastor, who can encourage you to grow in the things of God. There is so much more of God you can know. The more we know of God, we find out there is more, there is always more!

As a final thought I want to share the words of a song I wrote a number of years ago. I wrote it because this is my heart for you and I believe this is God's heart for you as well.

If I could just find some way to reach your heart,
I would tell about the love of God,

If I could swim all the oceans and reach for the stars,
If I could hear all the secrets, the secrets of God,
I would tell you about the love of God,

If I could just find some way to pull it all together for you,
I would cry all the mountains and the rocks would cry out for you,
If I could become a lamb like He did for you,
I would tell you about the love of God,

If I could reach to the heavens and swim to the depths of the sea,
If I had faith, I would touch the hem of his garment for you,
I would tell you about the love of God,

If I could just find some way to answer all your questions,
I would tell you about the mysteries and the wonders of God,

And the answers to your questions are written in the skies above, just like the wise men who followed, who followed that star,

And the answers to your questions are carried in the bowels of time, in the Ancient of Days you can find your peace of mind,

I would tell you about the love of God,

I see a picture of a lake made with diamonds and crystals, and all the answers to the questions of life can be found there,

I see a man like the son of God standing on the shore,

And He's clothed with glory and arrayed with Majesty,

And His beauty is such it would steal the heart,

I see the emptiness and the loneliness in His heart as He looks for you,

If I could just find some way to explain it somehow,

I would tell you about the love of God.

I know God is real and He wants to meet with you. Don't let your life go by without giving Him an opportunity to prove it!

Endnotes

1 Mahatma Ganhdi, *Multi-faith Service*, (Surrey: The Gandhi Foundation, 1983), gandhifoundation.org/multifaith.html, accessed 8/10/2007.

2 C.S. Lewis, *Surprised by Joy*, (London: Harvest Press, 1955).

3 George G. Hunter III, *How to Reach Secular People*, (Nashville: Abingdon Press), 1992, 24.

4 Hunter, 24.

5 Hunter, 31.

6 David J. Hesselgrave., *Communicating Christ Cross Culturally 2nd Edition, An Introduction to Missionary Communication*; (Zondervan: Grand Rapids, Michigan), 1991, 214.

7 Hunter, 13.

8 Hesselgrave, 217.

9 Eddie Gibbs, review of *Connecting with the Spirit of Christ: Evangelism for a Secular Age*, by Christopher C. Walker *Missiology*, (April 1990): 217, available from Academic Search Elite [database on-line]; http:/search.epnet.com (Boston, MA: EBSCO Publishing, accessed October 7, 2004).

10 Hunter, 46.

11 Robert G. Clouse, *Review of Atheism From the Reformation to the Enlightenment,* ed. by Michael Hunter and David Wooton *Church History* 64, No.1 (Mar 95):128, available from Academic Search Elite [database on-line]; http:/search.epnet.com (Boston, MA.: EBSCO Publishing, accessed February 14, 2004).

12 Clouse, 128.

13 Charles B. Paris, *Review of Atheism in France, 1650-1729,* by Alan Charles Kors. *Church History* 62, No.2 (Jun 93):272-273, available from Academic Search Elite [database on-line]; http:/search.epnet.com (Boston, MA.: EBSCO Publishing, accessed February 14, 2004).

14 Paris, 272.

15 Richard H. Popkin, *Review of At the Origins of Modern Atheism* by Michael J. Buckley *American Historical Review* 94, (Jun 89): 704.

16 Miceli, 4.

17 Miceli, 2.

18 Miceli, 17.

19 Millard Erickson, *Christian Theology,* (Grand Rapids: Baker Publishing Group, 1998), 179.

20 David Dorries, *Our Christian Roots Volume I,* (Broken Arrow, Oklahoma: Kairos Ministries International, 2002), 17.

21 Erickson, 201.

22 Joseph Free, *Archaeology and Bible History* (Wheaton, Illinois: Scripture Press, 1969), 1.

23 Nelson Glueck, *Rivers in the Desert* (New York: Farar, Straus and Cudahy, 1959), 136.

24 Gary Habermas and Antony Flew, *Did Jesus Rise From the Dead?* (San Francisco: Harper and Row, 1987), 43.

[25] Sir Frederic Kenyon, *The Bible and Archaeology* (New York: Harper and Row, 1940), 288.

[26] Kenyon, 289.

[27] Frederick P Fogle, *True Revival.* Union Gospel Press, *Gospel Herald and Sunday School Times*, 14, No. 2 (Spring Quarter: 1996): 1.

[28] Jessie Penn-Lewis, *The Awakening in Wales and Some of the Hidden Springs.* (Fort Washington PA: Christian Literature Crusade, 1993), Available from, http://www.revival-library.org/catalogues/world6/penn-lewis-awakening, Chapter 4, Accessed April 13,2001.

[29] Penn-Lewis, Chapter 4.

[30] David Matthews, *I Saw The Welsh Revival.* (Chicago: Moody Press,1951), 22-23.

[31] George Jeffreys, *Healing Rays.* (London: Elim, 1935), 55.

[32] Fogle 1996, 2

[33] Robert I. Bradshaw, *Bending The Church to Save the World: The Welsh Revival of 1904* (Mid Glamorgan: Evangelical Press of Wales. 1995), Available from http:/www.robibrad.demon.co.uk/Revival.htm, 3 accessed December 15, 2007.

[34] James A. Stewart, *Invasion of Wales by the Spirit through Evan Roberts*, (Asheville NC: Revival Literature, 1963), Available from:
http://www.gospelcom.net/glia/2001/volume02/rp_0180801.shtml, accessed December 15, 2007.

[35] Stewart, 1.

[36] Cornelius Van Til, *Christian Apologetics*, (New Jersey: P&R Publishing, 1976), 18.

[37] Hart, 235.

[38] Erickson, 586-593.

[39] Erickson, 602.

[40] Hart, 229.

[41] Hart, 220.

[42] Hart, 231.

[43] Jeffrey Palmer, *Paranormal Topics in the Media*, (Asheville NC: Revival Literature, 1963), Available from http://ezinearticles.com/?Paranormal-Topics-in-the-Media&id=82038, accessed December 15, 2007

[44] Mahatma Gandhi, *Mahatma Gandhi (1869-1948) Indian political and spiritual leader,* (The Quotations Page, 1994: http://www.quotationspage.com/quotes/Mahatma_Gandhi/ accessed 1/16/2008.

[45] Peter Kreeft, *What is God's Answer to Human Suffering?*, (New York: Peter Kreeft, 2008), http://www.peterkreeft.com/topics/suffering.htm, accessed January 16 2008.

[46] Martin Luther King, Jr., *Quotes*, (Quotes, 2001) http://www.funmunch.com/events/martin_luther_king_jr_day/martin_luther_king_jr_day_quotes.shtml, accessed January 16, 2008.

[47] William Wilberforce, *William Wilberforce Quotes*, (Thinkexist.com Quotations, 1999-2006): http://thinkexist.com/quotes/william_wilberforce/, accessed January 16,2008.

[48] Wilberforce, 1.

For more information:

Barry Raeburn Evangelistic Association
8988-L South Sheridan, Suite 254
Tulsa, Oklahoma 74133
info@barryraeburn.org
www.barryraeburn.org

2385644

Made in the USA